A Journey to the *High Places*

A Journey to the *High Places*

Hannah Hurnard's Spirituality and the Song of Songs

CHRISTOPHER FELIX BEZZINA

WIPF & STOCK · Eugene, Oregon

A JOURNEY TO THE *HIGH PLACES*
Hannah Hurnard's Spirituality and the Song of Songs

Wipf & Stock
An Imprint of Wipf and Stock Publishers
199 W. 8th Ave., Suite 3
Eugene, OR 97401
www.wipfandstock.com

ISBN 13: 978-1-62032-098-3
Manufactured in the U.S.A.

Grateful acknowledgment is made to my parents Michael and Lukarda Bezzina for their financial and emotional assistance. The author wishes to thank also Rev. Dr. Charlo Camilleri and Mr. Carmelo Muscat for proof reading this work and for providing academic counsel.

Contents

Foreword

IN CHAPTER 16 OF his book *Broken Hearts and New Creations*, titled "Brokeheart Mountain: Reflections on Monotheism, Idolatry, and the Kingdom," James Alison shares his reflections after participating in a pilgrim journey to the Holy Mountain Zion gone wrong, or at least not as expected. At the end of the chapter the author dreams of returning one day to the Holy Mountain with other pilgrims after having undergone

> an arduous process of learning in which we will have been stripped of different sorts of idolatry. A painful and disorienting process, for it is our hearts that will have become detached from forms of belonging to which they ought not to have been attached, so as to become aligned with something imperishable. On the way, we will have learned things about being human that none of us knew before, and what we know will be real. Our unity will no longer be that inspired by the fierce guardians of idolatrous righteousness. Our bonds will have become those of the broken-hearted.[1]

Hannah Hurnard, who spent sixteen years in the Holy Land, is one such transformed pilgrim who courageously underwent this arduous process and expressed her profound experience in writing. Journeying to those "High Places," she learned that on the mystical mountain only the honor and glory of the Lord dwell. As shown in this intertextual analysis, Hurnard's renowned allegorical novel *Hind's Feet on High Places*, written in 1955, is in line both with the biblical and mainstream Christian mystical tradition wherein the themes of transformation, journey, purification, change of heart, broken-heartedness, and ascent abound.

The conversion experience of 1924, which thrust her into a journey of trust and abandonment in God, was the first of many steps and experiences that opened her up to divine love. This experience triggered a three-fold dynamic process of transformation starting from (1) the coming out

1. J. Alison, *Broken Hearts and New Creations: Intimations of a Great Reversal* (London: DLT, 2010), 279.

of self-pity in the "valley of humiliation," (2) the escape from "fearings," (3) and the rapid ascent towards the "kingdom of love," "leaping on the mountains." Again, the distinction of the mystical journey in a tripartite process is itself a very classical metaphor. It is a process leading from darkness to light, from ignorance to wisdom, from the surface to the depths of our being, from illusion to truth. Hannah, while at once faithful to and transcending her religious tradition, delves into this process with much insight through knowledge of the sacred Scriptures and self-knowledge. She then expresses and communicates the truth she encountered through the allegorical literary form and method of writing.

This method becomes the space of encounter wherein people and their experiences meet, resonate, and relate in the light of God's self-revelation. In fact the communal and ecclesial space are necessary for a balanced and authentic interpretation of Scripture and of one's own spiritual journey inasmuch as "no prophecy of Scripture is matter of one's own interpretation" (2 Peter 1:20). The structured ecclesial community, or the church, laden with the wisdom of tradition and tried over the centuries through the historical vicissitudes, becomes the locus of support, challenge, and purification that protects both the individual and the faith sharing group from illusion, fundamentalism, or heterodoxy.

Unfortunately it seems that Hannah lacked this fundamental structure in her own journey. The Quaker tradition she was brought up in avoids the mediating agency between the worshiper and God, thus there is no guide to point out the way of a right or wrong way of practicing faith. Evangelicalism, which she embraced later in life, tends more toward the literal sense and interpretation of the sacred texts rather than the spiritual or allegorical. Frankly one can say that many of Hannah's shortcomings, as shown even in this work, could have been transcended with the support and the experience of the church nurtured by the presence of the incarnate Word in the words of the sacred texts and the bread of life, especially during the celebration of the divine liturgy, *fons et culmen* of the church.

Indeed the value of the present work, originally presented for an MA in Spirituality at the University of Malta, is primarily the contextualizing, through an intertextual interpretation, of Hannah's experience and texts using literature from the great Christian masters who, in virtue of their broken-heartedness, can show us the way in our adventure with God. This context provides, one may say, the spiritual-ecclesial communion of saints wherein the value and limits of Hannah and her experience could be tested in a balanced way.

The author provides the reader with an elegant and erudite structured text divided into four chapters. He paves our way through a minute exposition of *Hind's Feet on High Places* as an allegory in itself and then leads us to an intertextual analysis of the text and a study of the way Hannah uses the biblical text of the Song of Songs. Finally, he provides an in-depth analysis of Hurnard's own experience and the legacy she handed over to future generations.

The work is in itself an arduous process of learning on the intellectual and spiritual level. It avoids any positive or negative casual interpretation or judgment while opening up valid spaces for the reader and spiritual wayfarer to go beyond *Hinds' Feet* toward perfect love on the Holy Mountain, where all peoples and the whole of creation, transformed and broken-hearted, dwell in the presence of the Lord.

Charlò Camilleri, O.Carm.
Director of the Carmelite Institute Malta
Faculty of Theology
University of Malta

Introduction

WITH THE INCREASED ACCESS to knowledge and through the contribution of psychology in dealing with the processes of meaning, debates on spirituality have become very popular today. The individual yearnings toward the unsatisfied need is consistent with one's own existence. This includes an inquisitiveness toward the mysterious. Any advocated spirituality should aspire toward a relationship between the soul and the sacred.

Since the Second Vatican Council, when each individual has been urged to respond to the universal call to holiness, the concept of spirituality has become a fundamental term for Christians.[1] The yearning for the meaningful is evident everywhere, while the term "spirituality" stretches beyond any obvious religion. The spiritual antecedent in humans is a universal characteristic of every person.[2] However, this desire for true authenticity is not a recent discovery; its bedrocks are embedded in our traditions and history.[3] From the beginning of our existence the human person has exercised various ways and expressions to blend the compulsive force of ones own natural existence with the mysterious emotion. This analysis will essentially focus on Christian spirituality as a unique spirituality that we encounter today. As such, the subject matter of this book is related to the Christian religious experience. While this comprises any area of theology, this work is based primarily upon the relationship and personal aspect of the individual with the Holy Trinity. In particular, this relationship aspect will be considered through the use of allegory as a literal form applied by writers in their communication

1. See Vatican Council II, *Lumen Gentium* 39–42.

2. "Faith . . . is a universal human concern. Prior to our being religious or irreligious, before we come to think of ourselves as Catholics, Protestants, Jews or Muslims, we are already engaged with issues of faith. Whether we become nonbelievers, agnostics or atheists, we are concerned with how to put our lives together and with what will make life worth living. Moreover, we look for something to love that loves us, something to value that gives us value, something to honor and respect that has the power to sustain our being" (Fowler, *Stages of Faith*, 5).

3. See Gula, *Call to Holiness*, 1, 40–62.

of what is meaningful in their life. In the Bible, allegorical narratives are popular, such as the parables of Jesus, the Song of Songs, and the creation as portrayed in Genesis in the Old Testament. Moreover, even secular literature has incorporated the figurative language in their writings to express the dynamic relationship between God and the human being. Some famous allegorists include Prudentius (c. 348–413), Bernard Silvestris (1085–1178), John Milton (1608–74), Dante Alighieri (c. 1265–1321), John Bunyan (1628–88), George MacDonald (1824–1905), J. R. R. Tolkien (1892–1973) and C. S. Lewis (1898–1963).

Specifically, this book will analyse the spirituality of Hannah Hurnard (1905–90) by perusing her most famous allegorical narrative, *Hinds' Feet on High Places*, which has gone down well with people practically in every corner of the globe. In fact, her book has remained a bestseller until today. Few studies exist on this author; most focus mainly on her life. Another relevant point in this study is the use of allegory to narrate and put across Christian messages. In studying her spirituality, through an analysis of her allegorical narrative, this work will seek to underline the importance of the use of allegorical narratives to express one's own spiritual and religious experiences, and to see whether this style of writing could help readers to become more profound in their faith.

While reading *Hinds' Feet on High Places*, it is expected that we search for the message of the narrative from the text itself. The story contains various interpretations and, as readers, we are encouraged to comprehend these messages.[4] Despite this obvious conclusion, Hurnard's story is influenced by previous sources, knowingly or not. Whilst designing her narrative, different systems, traditions of meanings of texts, and her direct experience of life shadowed her literal composition. It is evident that the Bible was a fundamental stimulus, particularly the Song of Solomon. One cannot fail to notice the direct application of quotations and references from the Song of Solomon, and how a discreet verse from Habakkuk inspired her to structure her story this way. In this study one should have a thorough understanding of the connections between the Song of Solomon and her allegorical text in order to comprehend better the spirituality of Hannah.

The method which will be applied to understand more deeply Hurnard's spirituality, through *Hinds' Feet on High Places,* is known as

4. See Allen, *Intertexuality*, 62.

intertexuality.[5] By mapping the affinity between her narrative and the various sources we can strengthen our understanding of her narrative and integrate her spirituality in line with others. By using this procedure and by delving deeper in reaching a meaning, this work shows the connections between a text and others in conveying the same message.[6] The text itself can be termed as intertexual.[7] It is declaring that Hurnard, as author, selected her style of writing and conveyed certain messages from a previously developed frame of reference. Each symbol, story line, character, feature, and even the selected style of writing in Hurnard's allegory arises from different blends and assimilations within a range of literature.[8] No meaning is taken for granted until it is developed in the narrative itself and linked with other similar material.[9] Moreover, reference was made to Hurnard's books including her biography as this narrative is influenced by her experiences in life, pleasant or painful. Additionally, the identity of Hurnard as "subject of enunciation" is *lost* in the writings.[10] As Barthes says:

> The Author, when believed in, is always conceived of as the past of his own book: book and author stand automatically on a single line divided into a *before* and an *after*. The Author is thought to *nourish* the book, which is to say that he exists before it, thinks, suffers, lives for it, is in the same relation of antecedence to his work as a father to his child.[11]

When making use of intertexuality one has to be careful about the drift of the text. Although different texts may be connected someway or other, this connection should not substitute the general drift of the author's text through their interpretation. But on the other hand, one should accord their interpretation the due importance. While taking into consideration the link between Hurnard's text and other texts this study

---

5. See Orr, *Intexuality*. "Intertexuality, or the work of meaning through which one text in referring to another text both displaces this other text and receives from it an extension of meaning" (Ricoeur, *Figuring the Sacred*, 148).

6. See ibid., 148.

7. See Barthes, *Elements of Semiology*, 9, 67, 73.

8. See Kristeva, *Desire in Language*, 39; Ricoeur uses the term *metaphorized narrative*, 150.

9. See Allen, *Intertexuality*, 14.

10. See ibid., 40.

11. Ibid., 72.

will also focus on a coherent and subjective interpretation.[12] According to Kristeva's view on intertexuality we can produce a set of meanings in accordance with one's insight.[13] Due to the lack of research on Hurnard's spirituality this book would perhaps contribute to an acceptable level of understanding of her spirituality and accordingly provoke further analysis on this point. Moreover, by combining this process with Hannah's interpretation of the Song of Songs and other biblical sources this study hopes to understand better why later on she promotes a more universalistic approach to Jesus's salvation. Instead of pronouncing judgement on Hannah and her experience, this study aims at pinpointing the strengths presented in her spirituality and at the same time respecting her courage in what she was trying to promote.

As a consequence, this study will be split into four chapters. In chapter 1 the allegorical narrative is subjectively considered in all its aspects, and the central themes shall be laid out without any reference to other secondary connections. Chapter 2 will investigate the allegorical narrative by relating it with other literary works she published. These other narratives provide the tools through which Hannah's allegorical narrative could be constructed. Thus, chapter 2 shall present an intertexual analysis between her other publications and *Hinds' Feet on High Places*. Similarly, chapter 3 shall present another intertextual analysis between the many biblical abstracts and their relation to the narrative, in the hope of showing her biblical interpretations. Several spiritual themes, emerging from the preceding chapters, shall be discussed in chapter 4 to present a consistent spirituality. While presenting the themes, the strengths and weaknesses of Hannah's spirituality shall be related to other Christian spiritual traditions. However, for an effective comprehensive study the introductory section at the start of this study shall examine the significance of allegory and spirituality.

---

12. See Ricoeur, *Figuring the Sacred*, 150.

13. "The text is therefore *productivity*, meaning that (1) its relation to the language in which it is sited is redistributive (destructive-constructive) and consequently it can be approached by means of logical categories other than purely linguistic ones; (2) it is a permutation of texts, an intertextuality: in the space of a text, many utterances taken from other texts intersect with one another and neutralize one another" (Orr, *Intertexuality*, 27).

HANNAH HURNARD: LIFE AND WRITINGS

Hannah Hurnard's life can be described as a transformation from one extreme to the other. From a fragile and timid teenager to a strong-minded person, no longer was she dominated by hesitation and self-deprecation. She matured into an admirable woman of freedom and bearer of real love toward the world. Born to a wealthy family from Colchester, England, on May 31, 1904, she was the third child out of four. Her parents were staunch Quakers who believed in total separation from the world. Considering that period, the Hurnards were affluent. They resided in a ten-bedroom Hill House. About seven servants looked after Hannah's needs. Her parents, who were devoted aristocratic Quakers, spent most of their free time preaching and attending religious activities. Up to the age of nineteen Hannah was never happy. Her social context was limited due to the family's social status. Making friends was also a problem for her. Thus, her social life was very limited. She did attend school but couldn't frequent any public entertainment area on account of the rigid lifestyle the Hurnards believed in.

> Hannah's social status undoubtedly cut her off from most of her peers. Her mother came from the aristocracy: her father was "a gentleman of independent means," and in the early part of the twentieth century, such people did not mingle too readily with the "hoi polloi!" It was not a case of snobbery on one side, or subservience on the other: more a feeling that each person must fulfill the role assigned to him or her in life, and that society would fall apart unless everybody kept his place and did his duty.[14]

Her only refuge was in the surrounding countryside. To make matters worse, she had a stammering problem which made it difficult for her to communicate. It is no wonder that Hannah developed an aversion toward life and toward new public situations.[15] At the age of eleven she opted to accept Christ, in the hope of finding meaning to life, an option strongly recommended by her parents. However, Hannah still remained despond and dejected. Although Hannah perceived the vitality of her parents' and their friends' faith, she disliked their rigid puritan lifestyle imposed on her.[16] Hannah considered herself as being isolated from the freedom of

14. Wood, *Hannah Hurnard*, 27.

15. See Hurnard, *Hearing Heart*, 11.

16. "We hear much in these days of the unfortunate results of a Puritan upbringing,

the world. The only course recommended by her family was Jesus. But unfortunately this course didn't bring about any change in her life. In her own words, Hannah expressed, "God and the unseen world always seem so terribly unreal to me. I read the Bible and I do try to believe, but I never seem able to get into vital touch with God or hear His voice speaking to me personally."[17] Friends tried to exhort her to believe, yet all the possible procedures by her earnest evangelical friends were ineffective, and she no longer believed in the existence of a God.[18]

What transformed her life was an invitation by her father on July 26, 1924, to attend a Christian convention in Keswick Lake District which was held yearly. But she dreaded the meeting. She felt that place was not suitable for her. Her only haven was the surrounding countryside. She was dominated by this content. But during the last meeting of that convention something happened that transformed her life. During the convention parents were asked who was willing to send their children abroad as missionaries. On seeing her dad acceding to this proposal Hannah broke down in a state of bewilderment and sorrow. She ran to her room and knelt in her bedroom, sobbing sorrowfully.

> That was the last straw. I struggled to my feet and hurried out of the tent. Getting on my bicycle I tore back to our lodging-house outside the town, rushed into my little room, and locking the door fell on my knees beside the bed. And at last in an extremity of despair and misery of heart I cried out aloud, "O God, if there is a God anywhere, You must make Yourself real to me. If you exist and are really what these people describe You to be, You can't leave me like this."[19]

While she was kneeling and reading 1 Kings 18, Hannah experienced a conversion. "It was then that she read verse 38 with new eyes, for only Elijah stood alone and doused the altar with water, did the fire of the Lord fall. And the message struck home."[20] Enlightenment touched her heart

---

and in my own family we all experienced, as we grew to adolescence and adulthood, a most violent reaction and antagonism to this environment and outlook" (*Hearing Heart*, 9).

17. Ibid., 5.

18. Ibid., 10.

19. Ibid., 15.

20. Wood, *Hannah Hurnard*, 41; Hannah later used the spiritual experience from 1 Kings 18 and adopted it in chap. 1 of the allegorical narrative *Hinds' Feet* through the use of the altar and fire metaphor.

assuring her that God loved her even if she was timid, depressed, and had a stammering problem.[21] Finally, she was happy. From that moment, she kept on experiencing freedom and grace of God, and modifying her character intimately through his love.

After her renewal at the Keswick Convention, Hannah started studying the Scriptures at Ridgeland's Bible College[22] in southwest London. Hannah became self-confident, regained her health, and summoned up her courage. Together with her faith she managed to suppress her morbid thoughts. Now she confronted her fears with determination and positive thinking. At the age of twenty one, she left the Bible College and enrolled with the Friends Evangelistic Band (FEB), which today is called the Fellowship for Evangelising Britain's Villages.[23] The mission of the FEB was and still is to disseminate the Good News to the villages and houses of the United Kingdom. During her experience with FEB Hannah claimed that she felt infused with high spirits. Gone were her gloomy feelings. Although Hannah was living in a caravan, away from her comfortable house, she was more vivacious and happier. This made her parents proud of her conversion and of her role in sharing the Good News.

In 1930 Hannah was appointed deputation secretary of the Friends Evangelistic Band. In Ireland while she was evangelizing she experienced another call from God, a call which urged her to extend her missionary work to the Jews in Palestine. On pondering on this call she decided to affiliate with the British Jews Society, and in 1932 proceeded to Haifa in Palestine as a temporary teacher and nurse.[24] During her missionary work she realized that her call was actually to extend the gospel to the Jews. After a short stay in Switzerland, where she brushed up her German, in 1935 she moved to the Jewish Quarter in Jerusalem. At that time, Palestine was the scene of civil war. Moreover, Palestine saw a great influx

---

21. "He is real: He is here: He loves me: He actually loves me. I am perfectly safe" (Hurnard, *Hearing Heart*, 18).

22. See *All Nations Training Mission*.

23. "Our aim is to proclaim and live out the gospel of Jesus Christ in the villages of Britain, in order to establish effective Christian witness. We seek to encourage and enable village churches in Bible teaching, prayer, worship and evangelism" (*Fellowship for Evangelizing Britain's Villages*).

24. "CMJ, a dynamic ministry propelled by devotion to God and the fulfillment of His promises to His people Israel, is reaching out to thousands, both locals and visitors to the Land. The official website of today British Jews Society" (CMJ Israel).

of European Jews fleeing Germany under the terror of the Nazi regime. Accompanied by several colleagues she travelled far and wide to villages and camps in Palestine to assist both Jews and Arabs in those hard times. In her book *Wayfarer in the Land* she recounted all her experiences while serving as a missionary in Palestine.

In 1938 tension in Palestine heightened as plans of creating a unified Arab/Jewish state were being devised. Violence escalated against the British occupants. In fact, around the year 1946 kidnapping of English citizens by Jewish terrorists took place and Operation Polly came in effect. British citizens were evacuated from Palestine to Egypt and then repatriated. In 1947 Hannah traveled back to Jerusalem where she worked as a housekeeper despite her lack of housekeeping skills. In that same year the mandate of the British over Palestine expired and war broke out in Jerusalem between Jews and Arabs. She stayed at the Jewish Quarter in Jerusalem and narrated the experience of war in her book called *Watchmen on the Walls*. When war was over in 1948 Hannah took a holiday in Haifa. In 1949 she had to return to England as her father passed away. Later, Hannah returned to Palestine, but to her disappointment her missionary activities were wound up.

During a short holiday in Cyprus she received a new call to take up writing and to publish books.[25] In 1950 she published *Watchmen on the Walls*, and later her autobiography *The Hearing Heart*. Later, in 1954, she published two other books titled *The Kingdom of Love* and *God's Transmitters*. In 1954 after her visit to Switzerland she published her most famous book, *Hinds' Feet on High Places*, and *Mountain of Spices*. Sometime later she was criticized by evangelicals for diverging from orthodox theology, but Hannah adhered to her views. Universalist thoughts were laid to her charge. However, she kept exploring more. In 1957 she wrote *The Heavenly Powers* and *The Inner Man*, which dealt more with paranormal matters. In 1960 she moved to New Mexico, and on the Bible's inspiration she became a vegetarian. She strictly followed the vegetarian regimen to become later a fruitarian. Following some other traveling Hannah moved back to Hill House in 1984. In 1988 she published her last book, called *Thou Shalt Remember*, which is an autobiographical book covering her

---

25. Hannah Hurnard's style of writing is very much similar to the Quaker style of writing. Her way of writing can be called a journal, however it bears little resemblance either to diaries or to the practice of "journaling" which is common today. See Durham, *Spirit of the Quakers*, 50.

entire life. In 1989 Hannah was diagnosed with colon cancer, and a year later she passed away in Colchester.

ALLEGORICAL LANGUAGE AND SPIRITUAL EXPERIENCE

In the preface to her book *Hinds' Feet on High Places*, the author states that the subject treated in her allegorical narrative is inspired by the following biblical verses in the Old Testament:

"The voice of my beloved!
Look, he comes leaping upon the mountains,
bounding over the hills." (Song 2:8)
"God, the Lord, is my strength;
he makes my feet like the feet of a deer,
and makes me tread upon the heights." (Hab 3:19)
"He made my feet like the feet of a deer,
and set me secure on the heights."
(Ps 18:33)

Through her inspiration and inquisitiveness she delved deeper into the significance of these three biblical verses. While the scriptural verses could be considered allegorical in their literary form, in her narrative Hurnard exhibited her acumen into the inner meanings of these verses. In the preface, she anticipated our judgment and stated that her allegorical story is not a fictitious one. It had a deeper concreteness not to let others misinterpret her intentions, and she cited freely the narrative's general theme: to be able to "leap upon the mountains, skipping upon the hills." She depicted this power as the "victorious living," explaining that this desire to "leap" upon any obstacles and to reach union with God is the desire of all those who love Him. Prior to embarking on the analysis of what she means by this victorious living, one must expand on allegory as a literal and interpretive device, recognizing allegory's importance in Christian spirituality. Allegory, as a unique design of language, had been undervalued and misused continually. The reason of this distrust was due to its style, which was judged as an obstruction to a direct understanding of a text. The main argument against allegory was that it disregards literal reasoning. However such adverse marks, even though powerful during the early nineteenth century, were confronted by scholars such as C. S. Lewis

(1898–1963), Angus Fletcher, D. W. Robertson (1914–92) and Maureen Quilligan, among others.[26] Lately Pope Benedict XVI, in line with Vatican II's Dogmatic Constitution *Dei Verbum*, mainly through the publication of his work on the life of Jesus and also through the promulgation of the Apostolic Exhortation *Verbum Domini*, has pointed out the limits of the historical-critical method when it is presented as the only valid way of interpreting Scriptures.[27]

However, in the midst of this state of affairs a definition of allegory as a distinctive way of writing could not be given, and even if definitions were provided they risked exclusivity. It could be for this reason that when something cannot be clearly defined, it is regarded with prejudice and disapproval. Indeed, by its own nature allegory tends to slip away from any kind of strict definition.[28] Perhaps there is no definition of allegory, only examples and forms of writing which are somewhat allegorical. The traditional description of allegory, and its enmity, was that it placed one thing in the place of another (*a* meant *b*), and that this relationship is hypothetically organised.[29]

While allegory was viewed flippantly, realism as a literacy technique became the foremost form. However, the belief that realism was the only natural form of expression was questioned. Allegory, in our modern times, has recovered its importance, but not without adaptations to its understanding and usage.[30] Modern approaches toward allegory, especially those made by authors such as Walter Benjamin (1892–1940), Paul de Man (1919–83) and Northrop Frye (1912–91), are different from the traditional ways of composing and understanding allegory.[31] These authors advise us that all literature in its structures and substances is allegorical. Paul De Man considers this writing as a form of a disguise giving an

26. See Lewis, *Allegory of Love*; Fletcher, *Allegory*; Robertson, *Preface to Chaucer*; Quilligan, *Language of Allegory*.

27. See Vatican Council II, *Dei Verbum* 3; Benedict XVI, *Jesus of Nazareth*; idem., *Verbum Domini*; John Paul II, *Interpretation of the Bible*.

28. Jon Whitman stresses the fact that each text must be explored in its historical dimension, not only because the circumstances influenced the author, but allegory as a term meant different things for each period (Whitman, *Allegory*, 12).

29. "In the simplest terms, allegory says one thing and means another. It destroys the normal sequence we have about language that our words 'mean what they say'" (Fletcher, *Allegory*, 2; Whitman, *Allegory*, 2–3; Tambling, *Allegory*, 1–18).

30. See Fletcher, *Allegory*, 304–59.

31. See Benjamin, *Origin of German Tragic Drama*.

identity to the person. Focusing on autobiographies, which can be viewed as opposites of allegory, he describes these autobiographies as disfiguring, because no author can fully write about one's life while alive. Autobiographies can be associated with the symbols in Romanticism because when writing these narratives, the author needs the ability to see one's self in relation to a whole understanding of self-identity in relation to time.[32.] On the other hand, Northrop Frye looks at interpretation of texts from another angle and explains that when we interpret we are criticizing and this is a form of allegorising by making commentaries and rereadings of it. In a nutshell, a text shows that when we read a text, we do not read the text truly but our version of it. The meaning we attach to a text may be different than that which is expressed.[33]

As an original way of writing, allegory connotes a desire for clarity and truth. In delving deeper into matters one cannot keep away from the allegorical style. While language becomes an obstacle when we seek to understand matter more deeply, imagination becomes an instrument for the writer to describe that which cannot be explained in plain language.[34] Quoting Whitman, "Allegory turns its head in one direction, but it turns its eyes in another."[35] This is valid, because fiction, while it is committing itself to imaginative figures, is withdrawing us back to reality. Therefore, it is correct to say that allegory is full of secrets which are weaved with emotions. It is also a desire to understand reality and a curiosity toward the mystery.[36] The techniques applied by allegorists are various; the most

32. See De Man, *Allegories of Reading*, 221.

33. See Frye, *Anatomy of Criticism*, 15.

34. "By placing myself at the very heart of the act of reading, I am hoping to place myself at the starting point of the trajectory that unfolds itself into the individual and social forms of the imagination. In this sense, my approach does not exclude this other wholly different approach but leads to it" (Ricoeur, *Figuring the Sacred*, 145). "In German one of the terms for *imagination* is the compound word *Einbildunbskraft*: literally, the 'power (*Kraft*)' of 'forming (*Bildung*)' into 'one (*Ein*).' . . . Faith forms a way of seeing our everyday life in relation to holistic images of what we may call the *ultimate environment*. Human action always involves responses and initiatives. We shape our actions (our responses and initiatives) in accordance with what we see to be going on. We seek to fit our actions into, or oppose them to, large patterns of action and meaning" (Fowler, *Stages of Faith*, 24).

35. Whitman, *Allegory*, 2.

36. "'Allegory' derives from the Greek word 'allegoreo,' formed from 'allos' (other) and 'agoreuo' (to speak in a place of assembly, the 'agora,' the marketplace). The 'other meaning' of allegory may conceal a secret significance, in that it may persuade readers

common of them are similes, personification and metaphors.[37] In fact, allegory has been described as a sustained and developed metaphor into a narrative.[38]

Particular attention is to be accorded to Galatians 4:21–26 where Saint Paul gives prominence to allegorical interpretation. Also, Saint Paul interprets the Old Testament story of Abraham and his relationship with Hagar and Sarah allegorically. For Saint Paul, when this event is construed in this way it is perused and understood for its essential meaning. In this, the Apostle is introducing a new way of looking at historical events in the Old Testament as *foreshadowing* the New Testament (Col 2:17).[39]

On one hand, we have the literal interpretation, and on the other hand, we have what we can call a spiritual reading, which through the accession to *logos* enhances our apprehension of historical events.[40] This method is not discrediting the historical understanding of the events. On the contrary, Paul views the historical events in the Old Testament as matters of another time and which prefigure future things in relation to the *logos*. Hence, the historical narratives in the Old Testament can have both a literal and spiritual understanding.[41] It is through this same mentality that the Church has enriched itself with allegorical narratives of all sorts throughout its history.[42] Such allegorical narratives inspired from Scriptures should be considered as an expression of longing and of spiritual needs.[43]

---

to probe for another meaning, it may enrich the meaning that has been given, or it may draw attention to a split between the surface meaning and what is underneath" (Tambling, *Allegory*, 6; Lewis, *Allegory of Love*, 60; Gay, *Transformation of Allegory*, 11).

37. See Fletcher, *Allegory*, 3.

38. See Gay, *Transformation of Allegory*, 7.

39. Jeremy Tambling also mentions 2 Cor 3:13–16 where Saint Paul explains the meaning of the "veil" in Exod 34:29–35, "The veil was literally on Moses's face, but figuratively upon their hearts. When the heart of Israel converts to Christianity, that veil, says St Paul, will be taken away. It is Christianity, that it does not need a veil because the unfolding glory of Christ can be seen openly" (Tambling, *Allegory*, 29; Aers, *Piers Plowman*, 17).

40. See Tambling, *Allegory*, 16; Fletcher, *Allegory*, 21–22.

41. See Origen, *De principiis* 4.9.

42. See Fletcher, *Allegory*, 5.

43. Patricia Burke describes the imagination as an open doorway that directs and mediates experience of God that goes beyond images, beyond naming, and beyond language. Imagination helps individuals to integrate the felt sense of a divine presence into their lives (Burke, "Healing Power"; Fletcher, *Allegory*, 23.

What is significant at this stage is when allegorical interpretation should be used as a tool. Origen (c. 185–254) indicates certain examples in the Bible where allegorical interpretation might be valuable. He establishes his reasoning on the conviction that the whole of Scripture is divinely inspired. In support of his firm belief he refers to 2 Timothy 3:16: "All scripture is inspired by God and is useful for teaching, for reproof, for correction, and for training in righteousness."[44] This conviction impelled Origen to gain a fuller appreciation of those verses of Scripture which can be considered as irrelevant or difficult to comprehend. He presents instances where allegorical interpretation can provide us with enriching understanding of these puzzling texts. He mentions parables, texts which use metaphors, texts which are uneven with the authoritative instructions of God, texts which can be perceived as immoral, or when there is unconnected chain of events in a text's narrative.[45] For these texts Origen accredits the use of allegory and somewhat disregards the literal interpretation. Gregory of Nyssa (c. 335–94) also adheres to the use of allegorical interpretation in texts with ambiguous literal meaning.[46] For Gregory of Nyssa, such impossibilities of a coherent understanding of Scripture direct the reader to delve in the spiritual meaning of Scripture by employing allegory.[47] Allegory is then utilized to sustain a comprehensible theological perception of the scriptural texts and reaffirm Origen's and Gregory's principle that Scripture is integral and relevant to the reader's enlightenment. Therefore, even though allegory embeds a foreign allusion to the author's intentions on the text, it attempts to reapply the meaning of a scriptural text to the reader with one's own different context from the author.[48] It is by acknowledging this distinction of allegory that we can affirm that the reading of Scripture becomes quasi-sacramental because from the understanding of the text the reader is allowed to participate in the mystery of Christ.[49] Through allegorical interpretation one does

---

44. *Philokalia of Origen*, 27–28.

45. See Ludlow, "Theology and Allegory"; *Philokalia of Origen*, 51–53.

46. "Scripture 'teaches nothing but charity, nor condemns anything except cupidity, whatever appears in the divine Word that does not literally pertain to virtuous behavior or the truth of faith you must take to be figurative'" (Augustine, *On Christine Doctrine* 3.10, 15).

47. See the prologue to Gregory of Nyssa, *Great Catechism*.

48. See Ludlow, "Theology and Allegory," 61; Fowler, *Stages of Faith*, 26, 30.

49. See *Philokalia of Origen* 12.1–2. "The spiritual exercises of St. Ignatius of Loyola

not only seek to clarify the perplexity in specific narratives; allegorical interpretation inclines the reader to contemplate on Scripture in the light of their present experience.[50]

For this study, these principles are significant in analysing Hannah Hurnard's allegorical narrative. Hannah Hurnard perused and contemplated the scriptural texts. She used allegory both as an interpretive device in her texts and as a mode of construction to compose her narrative *Hinds' Feet on High Places*. The meanings from the Scriptures provided Hurnard's life with serenity, and as a result she was able to transcend God's salvific history to her personal life.

---

employ imagination. Reading here is not a process of understanding, it is more an exercise of praying and contemplation where the word of God intimately touches on the human soul" (Ward, "Allegoria"; Aers, *Piers Plowman*, 3; Ricoeur, *Figuring the Sacred*, 149).

50. Ricoeur, *Figuring the Sacred*, 144–66.

Chapter 1

The Allegory

Hinds' Feet on High Places

Most first time readers of Hurnard's narrative do not have any knowledge about the author's life, or about her other books in which she expounds her theology. Hence, in their approach to her narrative they do not have any preconceived opinions about Hannah Hurnard's own theology. Thus, this chapter will examine *Hinds' Feet on High Places* in all its respects without any reference to other secondary connections. One concludes that this analysis is subjective, since we are interpreting the narrative from a very subjective perspective. Surely, other readers will derive other messages from the narrative.

A technique to be used in the examination of *Hinds' Feet on High Places* is to divide the development of the story into sequential segments. This chapter splits the narrative into three parts: chapters 1–4 of the story will deal with Much-Afraid's context before setting out on the journey, while chapters 5–16 will focus on the journey up to its destination at the High Place, as explained later in chapters 17–20.

RESIDING AT THE VALLEY OF HUMILIATION

At the very start of the narrative, we are introduced to Much-Afraid, the main protagonist of the whole story. Only her name evokes what kind of person Much-Afraid is. A name conveys an identity. In this case a fearful personality is related to her name: "This is the story of how Much-Afraid escapes from her Fearing relatives and went with the Shepherd to the High Places where 'perfect love casteth out fear.'"[1]

Not only does one knows the name of the main character but also how closely she is related to the Fearings, and that her name was given by her family. She resided with the Fearings, and a bond was established among them. During her life Much-Afraid had only experienced fear. Brought up as an orphan in the house of her aunt, Mrs. Dismal Forebodings, she lived with her three cousins Gloomy, Spiteful, and Craven Fear.[2] Her upbringing and the present circumstances were influenced by the element of fear, symbolized in the characters. Her fearful attitude had been heightened by Mrs. Dismal Forebodings's pessimism, the despairs of Gloomy, the malicious character of Spiteful, and the constant bullying of Craven Fear. But the worst cousin was Craven Fear, "who habitually tormented and persecuted her in a really dreadful way." This is confirmed in the first chapter of the narrative when Craven Fear approached Much-Afraid and in turn bullied and controlled her.[3] His behaviour is really overbearing and repellent. On seeing him approaching she tried to hide away, but all in vain. Much-Afraid had no option but to protect herself. Despite her attempts to ignore him she surrendered to the intimidation. Being so fragile and frightful she ended up under his tormenting control.

> Her white face and terrified eyes immediately had the effect of stimulating Craven's desire to bait her. Here she was, alone and completely in his power. He caught hold of her, and poor Much-Afraid uttered one frenzied cry of terror and pain.[4]

The Shepherd is presented as the antithesis of Much-Afraid's relatives. Thus, her life is subjected to a conflict imposed by two opposite characters. On one hand, we find the Shepherd who is kind hearted, while on the other hand we encounter the Fearing Relatives with their repulsive character. Her relatives' rage against her employment with the Shepherd, the employment of which is deemed a great violation of their principles, reflects their character. To segregate her from the Shepherd, a marriage

---

1. Hurnard, *Hind's Feet*, 17.
2. Ibid., 18.
3. Ibid., 19.
4. Ibid., 32.

plan between Much-Afraid and Craven Fear was excogitated by the Fearing relatives.

> Like most of the other families who lived in the Valley of Humiliation, all the Fearings hate the Chief Shepherd and tried to boycott his servants, and naturally it was a great offence to them that one of their own family should have entered his service. Consequently they did all they could both by threats and persuasions to get her out of his employment, and one dreadful day they laid before her the family dictum that she must immediately marry her cousin Craven Fear and settle down respectably among her own people.[5]

The Fearings' aspiration to separate her entirely from the Shepherd could be perceived throughout her journey from the Valley of Humiliation until the High Places. Even before she set out in her journey threats were levelled at her. When the Fearings invaded her house, their aim was clear: to abduct her and then compel her to marry Craven Fear. This intrusion is described in chapter 2 of the narrative when Lord Fearing, Coward, and Gloomy were present. Lord Fearing tried to deceive her to wed her cousin and adopted a tactic different from that of Craven Fear. He wasn't domineering, but on the contrary reassured her of his care and attention. But soon one realized his clever trick. Seeing how dismayed and bewildered Much-Afraid was, the Fearings, led by Lord Fearing, assaulted her. They bolted the door. Now she found herself locked inside. When she tried to call for help Coward put his hand over her face, and she fainted due to lack of air. While in bed it was Gloomy's responsibility to watch over her, while the others plundered her food.[6] This scene brought out the fact that whenever the Fearings exerted greater control on Much-Afraid, she was bruised, tormented, frustrated, and humiliated by their deeds.

But this was not the only episode in Much-Afraid's life. Something else, more personal, threatened her life. She was crippled and had a crooked mouth. These physical defects were affecting her efficiency in her work, and her way of communication. Moreover, these defects sapped her morale and transformed her into a fearful person. But in spite of these physical hindrances and low self-esteem, she was employed at the Shepherd's, where her crooked mouth was perceived as a scandal by those who

---

5. Ibid., 15.
6. Ibid., 39–43.

were also at his service.[7] To make matters worse, the Fearings exacerbated the adverse effects of her physical weaknesses.

These circumstances accounted for Much-Afraid's desire to escape from the Valley of Humiliation. It was a story of conflict. There was little chance of escape, only slavery and confinement. An inner motive also impelled her to escape. She wished to be surrounded with happiness and encouragement. Her only course was to escape. But her physical limitations were hindering her work, and she "earnestly longed to be completed from these shortcoming and to be made beautiful."[8] Much-Afraid considered the Shepherd as the only one who could grant her true freedom and happiness. In fact, the name Shepherd depicted a caring and concerned person toward his sheep. He was the one that provided sustaining pasture and protection from adversity and guidance, and led his sheep to the High Places.

The High Places were the entire contrast with the Valley of Humiliation. This was the wider context where Much-Afraid resided. Her escape was not only from her relatives but also from the Valley of Humiliation, where only degradation and horrid conditions prevailed. The place to be sought was the High Places or the Kingdom of Love. In other words, her escape from the despair of the valley might lead her to a higher realm of appreciation and authentic life. This was the world of Much-Afraid; internally she was tormented with the mental distress caused by her physical defects, while in her immediate environment she was affected with the negative attitudes of her relatives. The fusion of these two elements represented the conditions of the Valley of Humiliation. It was from all these conditions that Much-Afraid sought to escape. Her only refuge was the Shepherd.

The struggles which Much-Afraid had to face led her to cry for remedy. Much-Afraid regarded the Shepherd as the protector, the one who would relieve her from the misery of her relatives and from her weaknesses. Nothing in her conscious mind suggested a genuinely meaningful life. All things appeared dull and debased her dignity. Despite the fact Ms. Valiant was deemed a determined woman who was not afraid of the Fearings, when Much-Afraid yelled for help Ms. Valiant's intervention was not enough to save her from her misery. While yearning to be the

7. Ibid., 18.
8. Ibid.

master of her difficulties, Much-Afraid wished to be able to leap from the mountains she encountered. Seeing Much-Afraid in such a state, Ms. Valiant was on the point of rebuking her. But soon she understood that what Much-Afraid needed was the Shepherd's mercy and assistance. Being near the Shepherd, Much-Afraid cried out:

> "What shall I do?" she cried as she ended the recital. "How can I escape? They can't really force me to marry my cousin Craven, can they? Oh!" she cried, overwhelmed again at the very thought of such a prospect, "its dreadful enough to be Much-Afraid, but to think of having to be Mrs. Craven Fear for the rest of my life and never able to escape from the torment of it is more than I can bear."[9]

The Shepherd reassured and comforted her. "Do not be afraid," he told her. He did not blame her for the problems she faced but supported her in her appeal to escape from the Valley. She realized that "as long as I [she] live in the Valley I [she] cannot escape meeting them [Fearings]."[10] At this stage we saw a Shepherd who is compassionate to Much-Afraid. He empathised with her and approved her decision to escape. The Shepherd's answer was to invite her to the High Places. He never dictated anything to her, but always invited her to take up his suggestions. While she viewed the proposal to escape to the High Places with ambiguity and hopelessness, she recognized that this journey was perilous due to her physical defects. Moreover, she realised her disfigurement was a handicap to be permitted to enter the High Places. This apprehension on the part of Much-Afraid was seen through by an empathizing Shepherd. While inviting her again he stressed that change was not impossible. He would offer her assistance to gain "hinds' feet" and to perform her duties satisfactorily: "How is it possible? And what would the inhabitants of the Kingdom of Love say to the presence of a wretched little cripple with an ugly face and a twisted mouth, if nothing blemished and imperfect may dwell there?"[11]

Certainly, the change was necessary. This was achieved by drinking from the streams of the High Places. However, Much-Afraid still found it difficult to risk, but the Shepherd assured her that she would be changed

9. Ibid., 20.
10. Ibid., 21.
11. Ibid., 23.

completely, even her name. "Are you willing to change completely, Much-Afraid, and to be made like the new name which you will receive if you become a citizen in the Kingdom of Love?"[12] This invitation, offered freely by the Shepherd, left Much-Afraid in a state of excitement. She accepted forthwith. A change of name meant that her whole personality would embrace a new form. Her identity would be transformed into something closely related with the Kingdom of Love.

A dynamic progress was being made. In order to be transformed into a new person Much-Afraid needed to emerge from her immediate cynical context, focusing specifically on reaching the High Places. Only by doing so, Much-Afraid would become a new creature. The only way to transform her crooked feet into hinds' feet and to change her identity was to reject the Valley of Humiliation and to ascend the mountain. Despite her compliance to journey to the High Places, she had to accede to another request prior to entering the Kingdom of Love. This was the flower of love. "Again he smiled, but added gravely, 'there is still one thing more, the most important of all. No one is allowed to dwell in the Kingdom of Love, unless they have the flower of Love already blooming in their hearts. Has Love been planted in your heart, Much Afraid?'"[13] Searching her heart she realized how her yearning to be loved differed from what the Shepherd foresaw.

> I think that what is growing there is a great longing to experience the joy of natural, human love and to learn to love supremely one person who will love me in return. But perhaps that desire, natural and right as it seems, is not the Love of which you are speaking? . . . I see the longing to be loved and admired growing in my heart, Shepherd, but I don't think I see the Kind of Love that you are talking about, at least, nothing like the Love which I see in you.[14]

A contrast between Much-Afraid's natural love and the Shepherd's way of loving was perceived. Much-Afraid's natural longing to be loved demanded transformation as well but this effort entailed faith, suffering, and sorrow. "'But it is so happy to love,' said the Shepherd quietly. 'It is

12. Ibid., 24.
13. Ibid.
14. Ibid., 24–25.

happy to love even if you are not loved in return. There is pain too, certainly, but Love does not think that very significant."[15]

Not comprehending the spirit of the Shepherd's words, she still trusted him and cooperated to be implanted by the seed of Love, but under a condition: to be loved in return. On implanting the seed of Love in her heart she experienced a sensation tinged with pain. This feeling imbued her with vitality. Henceforth, Much-Afraid underwent an inner transformation. When the Fearings invaded her house and constrained her to ignore the Shepherd's call to start the journey, the seed of love supplied her with the courage to rise from her miserable state and search the Shepherd. The seed of Love forced her to go beyond her fears. In the depth of night, she searched the Shepherd, hopefully still on time to begin the journey. Through the power of the seed of love already a gradual transformation took place in Much-Afraid, even if she was still in the Valley of Humiliation. However, she couldn't be fully transformed if she remained at this dreadful Valley. Finding the Shepherd at her side during her suffering and pain she cried out, "O my Lord, take me with you as you said. Don't leave me behind," and the Shepherd initiates the journey.[16]

ESCAPE FROM THE FEARINGS

During her ascent Much-Afraid was first accompanied by the Shepherd and later by the appointed guides who were waiting for her. She had to accept that for most of the time the Shepherd would not be present for the journey. But he made it clear that two companions had been selected to conduct and protect her. Had he been constantly present she wouldn't have develop hind's feet, moreover, the seed of love wouldn't have blossomed into a flower.[17] Reassuring her he said: "Remember, even though you seem to be farther away than ever from the High Places and from me, there is really no distance at all separating us."[18] Indeed, the seed of love would gradually grow in Much-Afraid and would open a new dimension of understanding the true love.[19] By travelling with the two guides Much-

15. Ibid., 25.
16. Ibid., 54.
17. Ibid., 63.
18. Ibid., 93.
19. "Only Love can really understand the music and the beauty and the joy of all

Afraid would be able to reach the High Places, develop hinds' feet, and learn new love. What the Shepherd solicited was her trust.[20]

The guides were obedient and faithful to the Shepherd's services. He would arrive to assist them instantly at their request. The two companions' names were Suffering and Sorrow, and Much-Afraid was apprehensive of their names. Suffering and Sorrow were twins, but not like Much-Afraid. They were perceived as strong, but she was perplexed by their mysterious demeanour. Also, she could not communicate with them due to a dialect problem. Indeed her trust in the Shepherd's selection of guides was dented. Her reaction was, "I can't go with them . . . I can't! I can't! O my Lord Shepherd why do you do this to me?"[21] The Shepherd, faced by Much-Afraid's lack of trust in him, reminded her of the promise she gave. He affirmed that either she trusted in him, or she had no choice but to return to the Valley. "You remember your promise, to accept the helpers that I would give, because you believed that I would choose the very best possible guides for you. Will you still trust me, Much-Afraid?"[22] Much-Afraid pondered her dilemma. But then she remembered that others had already made this journey and their experience was beneficial.[23] Convinced, she regained faith and agreed to proceed with them.

Undeniably, the journey wasn't plain sailing for Much-Afraid. She limped through the rocky tracks, and for most of the time Suffering and Sorrow had to lift her. Strangely, she felt that whenever she grasped their hands a painful pang ran through her spine, yet it gave her strength and courage to keep on walking.[24] Yet, there was something else threatening her progress. Her Fearing Relatives did not give up their plan to separate her from the Shepherd. Indeed, back at the Valley of Humiliation all the Fearing Clan agreed to stop and capture her. But they knew they couldn't maltreat her as the Shepherd wouldn't let them. They had no other option

---

created things. Have you forgotten that two days ago I planted the seed of Love in your heart?" (ibid., 61).

20. Ibid., 64.

21. Ibid., 66.

22. Ibid., 65–66.

23. "Others have gone this way before me . . . and they could even sing about it afterward" (ibid., 68).

24. Ibid., 71, 80.

but to convince her to change course and give up. They sent a group of Fearings to find her and to bring her back.[25]

Among the group was Pride, specifically chosen to be the first enemy because unlike Craven Fear he was attractive, tenacious, and never accepted a defeat. Much-Afraid was very surprised at Pride's approaches. Usually he disdained her with haughty looks, yet today he acted differently. Pride was amicable in his speech disclosing how dreadful this journey was. Flattery was the way he used to convince her to stop. Much-Afraid ceased to hold Sorrow and Suffering's hands and Pride took the opportunity and grabbed her hand. Then she comprehended his true purpose. In her heart and mind, she questioned the Shepherd and even her choice of going up to the High Places. What Pride affirmed seemed credible. Now she was tormented listening to Pride's discouragement and almost agreeing with his advice. In her confusion she saw a vision of the Shepherd singing to her a song. In that precise moment she cried for him and the Shepherd appeared. Pride was beaten with a staff and ran away. The Shepherd reproached her and asked her why she did not hold Sorrow and Suffering's hands, but Much-Afraid was unable to answer. Through her mistake she later noted that her pain exacerbated when holding again the hand of Suffering and Sorrow.[26]

While walking out of the Valley of Humiliation, Much-Afraid received the first lesson of her journey. In the presence of the Shepherd she observed wild flowers and appreciated their beauty at the same time. She wondered why these beautiful flowers lay in the wild where they're not appreciated.[27] However, the Shepherd showed her something novel, that is, true love which is offered unconditionally. The flowers were an example of humbleness given to anyone, without worrying who appreciated them or not. According to the Shepherd nothing was wasted. The flowers offered love, even if not loved in return. Moreover, the Shepherd concluded that even if one appreciated something, one did not grasp its beauty completely; he could only admire its aesthetic quality. For the Shepherd the hidden life of the soul was like a garden where he stepped in:

25. Ibid., 72–73.

26. Ibid., 75–76.

27. "They have so much beauty and sweetness to give and no one on whom to lavish it, nor who will even appreciate it" (ibid., 56).

> Nothing my Father and I have made is ever wasted . . . and the little
> wild flowers have a wonderful lesson to teach. They offer them-
> selves so sweetly and confidently and willingly, even if it seems
> that there is no one to appreciate them. . . . It is so happy to love,
> even though one is not loved in return. . . . All the fairest beau-
> ties in the human soul, its greatest victories, and its most splendid
> achievements are always those which no one else knows anything
> about, or can only dimly guess at.[28]

This was the Shepherd's celebrated truth: to pour oneself, to give
continuously even if this leads to no gain. Much-Afraid's eyes revealed
that the surrounding nature was governed by this law. She listened to a
new language of the birds, flowers and water. All sang songs convinced to
give themselves: "This is the law by which we live—it is so sweet to give
and give."[29]

Amid these achievements fraught with obstacles, Much-Afraid
faced a bigger dilemma which dented her faith. She had to accept detours
which were diverging from the Kingdom of Love. These detours confused
her greatly, and she had no option but to obey the Shepherd's choice. Her
state of shock and terror resulted in viewing these detours as contradictions, but the Shepherd explained that the detours were only postponements. However, her impatience impeded her from arriving at critical
judgement. Whenever Much-Afraid was experiencing a sense of anxiety
and doubt, the Shepherd always put his questions based on love. Indeed,
he asked: "Much-Afraid, do you love me enough to accept the postpone-
ment and the apparent contradiction of the promise, and to go down
there with me into the desert?"[30] At the Shepherd question she answered:

> I do love you, you know that I love you. Oh, forgive me because I
> can't help my tears. I will go down with you into the wilderness,
> right away from the promise, if you really wish it. Even if you can-
> not tell me why it has to be, I will go with you, for you know I do
> love you, and you have the right to choose for me anything that
> you please.[31]

Yet expressing these words were not enough, and whenever the Shepherd demanded something difficult and painful, Much-Afraid expressed

28. Ibid., 56–57.
29. Ibid., 61.
30. Ibid., 83.
31. Ibid., 83.

her struggles in symbolic ways through two ways: by building altars and by picking memorial stones.

Through the use of altars she surrendered her anxiety and her will. She was submissive, humble and obedient, and relied on the Shepherd's options. Her memorial stones acted as reminders of those tough moments which were later transformed into something new. Her love toward the Shepherd urged her to build altars, while every stone picked reminded her of these hard moments.

During the journey Suffering, Sorrow, and Much-Afraid diverged into a desert known later as Egypt. In this lifeless desert she found true love. In Egypt the Shepherd revealed to her the way things were refined. Accompanied by him she observed three types of works: the process of flour production—the grinding and sifting of wheat to produce this commodity; the potters art and workmanship in the creation of different objects from clay; and lastly 'smelting of gold in the furnace and the way it was refined. At that particular place she listened to the Shepherd uttering to her these words:

> See . . . how various are the methods used for grinding the different varieties of grain, according to their special use and purpose. . . . I bring my people into Egypt [desert] that they too may be threshed and grounded into the finest powder and may become bread corn for the use of others. . . . Cannot I do with you, Much-Afraid as this potter? Behold, as the clay is in the hand of the potter so are you in my hand. . . . My rarest and choicest jewels and my finest gold are those who have been refined in the furnace of Egypt.[32]

There and then she realized that the Shepherd would be moulding her into a new person, refining her into a lovely jewel. Faced by this revelation, Much-Afraid found the first "alphabet" of the Shepherd's love. Being symbolized in a flower Much-Afraid asked its name. The answer was: "Behold me! My name is Acceptance-with-Joy."[33] She understood the meaning of all the work she saw in the desert. By picking a pebble she remembered all the teachings in the desert and said, "He has brought me here when I did not want to come for his own purpose, I, too will look up into his face and say, 'Behold me! I am thy little handmaiden

32. Ibid., 88–90.
33. Ibid., 91.

Acceptance-With-Joy."[34] She lived up to Acceptance-with-Joy in the divergences that followed at the Shores of Loneliness and the Old Sea Wall. In the presence of Suffering and Sorrow, the Shepherd appealed to her to trust and obey his judgements.[35] Much-Afraid faced her loneliness. Rather than giving in, Much-Afraid was hopeful, remembering the workmen at Egypt and the fruits of their labour. Indeed, this could be viewed by her initiative to build another altar and offering her loneliness; "O my Lord! . . . I thank thee for leading me here. Behold me, here I am, empty . . . but waiting thy time to be filled to the brim with the flood-tide of Love."[36]

At the Shores of Loneliness and the Old Sea Wall the Shepherd was not present, and the Fearings took advantage of this moment to test her again. This time Pride was not alone but with others, including Resentment, Bitterness, and Self-pity. Not only did they discourage her to stay with the Shepherd, but above all they alleged in a high voice that the Shepherd was abusing her weakness. In such a situation she demanded to be taken to the High Places immediately. However, Much-Afraid was going through a change. Rather than give in to their calls, she picked a piece of rock and hurled it at them. Yet the Fearings did not give up hope. As she departed from Sorrow and Suffering they assaulted her. She tried to offer resistance. However, Pride attempted to capture her again. Faced by this situation she cried and asked for the Shepherd's assistance. Again it was he who saved her.

What caused her to drift away from Sorrow and Suffering was her impatience. Yet through her motivation, mistakes, and tests she fulfilled what she saw and promised in Egypt. Prior to crossing the Old Sea Wall she constructed an altar to offer her will, which had been tainted with bitterness.[37] All these delays reached a climax when the Seed of Love grew into a small bud surrounded by leaves. It was here that Acceptance-with-Joy bloomed in her heart, and again she offered part of her self to the Glory of God. She realized that whatever the Shepherd decided, even if it appeared contradictory and hurtful, was intended to give Glory to the Son of God. Now she experienced a new joy.

34. Ibid.
35. Ibid., 93.
36. Ibid., 97.
37. Ibid., 109.

At this point, she was ready to make the last part of the journey leading to the High Places ahead. Now there were no more divergences. She first reached the foot of the mountain, and later the Great Precipice, a Dark Forest immersed in mist, and the Valley of Loss. Now she had to face the perils posed by the journey's terrain and weather. Her enemies still lurked to persuade her, but now Much-Afraid was sharper witted.

Much-Afraid had to climb a precipice through a narrow, slippery, and very steep track. Gripped by terror, again she called her Shepherd. She couldn't make out why she had to go through such dangerous places. Again the Shepherd reassured her that such a climb might seem perilous, but it was not so. She built another altar and again laid down her will. True, the track was slippery and steep, but finally she arrived at a cave to rest. There she found another flower, symbolizing the second "alphabet" of love.

> My name is "Bearing-the-Cost," but some call me "Forgiveness." . . . I have borne and have not fainted; I have not ceased to Love, and Love helped me push through the crack in the rock until I could look right out onto the Love the sun himself. See now! There is nothing whatever between my Love and my heart, nothing around to distract me from him. He shines upon me and makes me rejoice, and has atoned to me for all that was taken from me and done against me.[38]

The dangerous paths she had to follow taught her this new lesson of love. Bearing ones crosses given by the Shepherd was a necessity. She had to bear the consequences, because she loved him in the knowledge that the Shepherd had already atoned her through his Grace. The difficult terrains signified that she had to learn to bear whatever the Shepherd presented to her. Through the reassurance of the Shepherd she reached the Dark Forest. Again and again Much-Afraid built altars and sacrificed her will, but she was still finding it difficult to trust the Shepherd. When thunderstorms broke out, she cowered but remained hopeful. She said to herself aloud, "I shall not die, but live and declare the works of the Lord."[39] Refuge was found in a hut during the thunderstorm. In these circumstances, the Shepherd had provided her with different means how

38. Ibid., 137–38.
39. Ibid., 149.

to sustain her in these difficult moments; he had given her miracle water, healed her injuries, and also provided safe places to relax.

After the storm abated the mist got denser. Much-Afraid was afraid that she might lose her way. Enemies tried to trick her, but she stayed on the path, even if not recognizing her whereabouts. She stayed with her guides, holding hands and singing a song dispelling negative thoughts about her relatives. When the Shepherd appeared, the mist cleared up. He led her to The Valley of Loss. Descending there, she lost the course. She had to lose everything and consequently she was bewildered about this. Faced with this situation she thought out whether to cease following the Shepherd, but she remembered that without his presence she would not be loved. On that moment she cried out what the Shepherd was longing to hear from the start:

> You may ask anything—don't let me leave you. Entreat me not to leave thee not to return from following after thee. . . . If you deceive me, my Lord, about the promise and the hinds' feet and the new name or anything else, you may, indeed you may; only don't let me leave you.[40]

On hearing these words, the Shepherd reminded her that whatever was happening was for the Glory of God. He also repeated what he had told her during the journey, to trust in his judgments. Indeed he said:

> Will you bear this too, Much-Afraid? Will you suffer yourself to lose or to be deprived of all that you have gained on this journey to the High Places? Will you go down this path of forgiveness into the Valley of Loss, just because it is the way that I have chosen for you? Will you still trust and still love me?[41]

On acceding to his request with conviction, she truly understood the Shepherd's purpose. No blemish could find its way into the High Places, and this applied also to her. This Valley of Loss led her to the conclusion that she had to lose everything, and then the Shepherd would purify her desires. Her sins, which were rooted in her nature, had to be purged. She crossed the Valley of Loss where the Shepherd led her to the boundary of the High Places. Although she limped and still had a crooked mouth, she was glad to be soon purified from her blemishes. He took her to the summit where he was transfigured before her. Together with Suffering

40. Ibid., 173.
41. Ibid., 174.

and Sorrow they worshiped him, and then with a pair of tongs the Shepherd took a piece of burning coal from a golden altar and touched Much-Afraid. While doing so he uttered, "Lo! This hath touched thy lips; and thine iniquity is taken away, and thy sin purged (Isa 6:6–7).''[42]

She experienced a new sensation. A flame flashed through her and she fainted due to its power. Waking up in the middle of night, she proceeded with the last part of her journey to which the Shepherd alluded to a burial place. In fact, the voice of the Shepherd did awaken her to find an altar and sacrifice her own longing to be loved in return. In the chilly night she sought the place of sacrifice. All of a sudden the noise of avalanches was heard and Sorrow and Suffering fearfully suggested to her to retreat, but Much-Afraid for the first time in her entire journey did not agree and proceeded ahead. They found refuge in a cave while the avalanches swept everything away.

In the cave she experienced a great dilemma. She had to offer her human natural love, but it was difficult for her because it was deeply rooted in her desires. Nonetheless, she had to offer it because the Shepherd demanded it. She took out the memorial stones and visualized all the stages of the journey there and then, and how the Shepherd treated her in each moment. At first, she thought of abandoning everything and to stop following the Shepherd. However she couldn't do this because at the core of her heart she knew that in every moment of hardship the Shepherd assisted and loved her more than any person in her world.

After the deluge Much-Afraid continued to search for the altar. She arrived at a grave-like grove. On descending she found the altar and a priest standing near it. She knelt down and called the Shepherd, but to her surprise he did not appear. Perplexed, she thought how she could get rid of the deep rooted human love in her body. This was impossible to her. So she decided to climb on the altar and let the priest tear her human love from her heart. In fact, that's what she did. On penetrating her heart with his steel hands the priest tore apart the natural human love, and fire descended to burn this love (1 Kings 18:30–39). The priest said, "Yes, it was ripe for removal, the time had come. There is not a rootlet torn or missing."[43] Exhausted, Much-Afraid fainted and slept. Her journey came to an end.

42. Ibid., 192.
43. Ibid., 214.

WHERE "PERFECT LOVE CASTETH OUT FEAR"

On waking up Much-Afraid found herself covered with luscious perfumes. She felt hearty and radiant. Thoughts about her previous night when she sacrificed herself on the altar came into her mind. Stupefied, she examined her breast for any signs of wounds or bruises, but found she was healed. Her body was in good shape. However, something changed in her. Her carnal love was extinguished. She left and observed her surroundings. What she saw was the altar covered with bright sunlight and some birds resting on it chirping. Below the altar flowed a stream leading to some bushes and the trees beyond. Everything looked resplendent and divine. She glanced at the stream and immersed herself in it. The water replenished her with energy. Regaining her health, she felt full of vigour.

Bathing in the sun, she caught sight of her feet. They weren't crooked anymore, but transformed into straight, elegant legs. To her astonishment she jumped joyfully in the stream. The promise was fulfilled; she now had hinds' feet. Even her twisted mouth was transformed. Looking at her reflection in a small, still pond, she looked relaxed and had a perfect face. Joyfully she spent the entire day bathing in the stream, eating fruits, sleeping, and enjoying the serenity of her surroundings. Being so happy, she was not even concerned about her future. She simply lived for the present moment.[44]

Three days elapsed, and on each day she was no longer subject to stress and enjoyed her reward. After sunset she was summoned by the Shepherd. She had leapt to a higher place, part of the Kingdom of Love. It was so easy for her to leap now. On seeing a hart climbing the great canyon walls, she leaped and followed them until she reached the ledges of the wall. The Shepherd was at the summit calling her on. Seeing her he shouted: "You—with the hinds' feet—jump over here."[45] Springing she landed beside him. He was dressed in royal purple robes and crowned. Indeed, the Shepherd was the King of the High Place. Smiling and proud of her he uttered:

> At last . . . at last you are here and the "night of weeping is over and joy comes to you in the morning" . . . this is the time when you are to receive the fulfilment of the promises. Never am I to

44. Ibid., 217–22.
45. Ibid., 225.

call you Much-Afraid again. . . . From henceforth you are Grace and Glory.[46]

The promise of a new name was fulfilled too. She was now to be known as Grace and Glory. No longer was she the person full of fear and hesitation, but now she was a person who had experienced grace and its glory. Now she was truly a transformed person. In her heart lay the flower from the thorn-shaped seed that the Shepherd had planted at the Valley of Humiliation. The thought of Longing-to-be-Loved had been dispelled to be replaced with the real love.

Grace and Glory realized that the priest at the altar was in fact the Shepherd himself. The Shepherd bowed his head and she kissed his hands. Only he could deliver her from the sins and corrupt desires. Yet, the Shepherd reminded her of another important promise to be fulfilled. "And now for the promise . . . that when Love flowers in your heart you shall be loved again. . . . Give me the bag of stones of remembrance that you have gathered on your journey, Grace and Glory."[47] She emptied her bags. Not stones came out of the bag but precious jewels. Twelve stones were changed into exquisite jewels which reminded her of the glorious moments of her journey. The King fixed the jewels on a circular band and crowed her as a princess of the Kingdom of Love (2 Tim 2:5).[48] As befitted a princess the King put two handmaidens at her service, Sorrow and Suffering. As they approached her, Grace and Glory observed their radiant faces for the first time. They were taller and stronger than Grace and Glory and even they had other names. Now their names were Peace and Joy. They kissed and hugged each other, and joyful Peace and Joy proclaimed, "Now we are to be your companions and friends forever."[49]

From that moment, Grace and Glory, Peace, and Joy remained together. They followed Grace and Glory wherever she went bringing joy

46. Ibid., 226.

47. Ibid., 228.

48. This echoes the mystical phenomenon referred to by women mystics like Teresa of Jesus and Mary Magdalena de' Pazzi (1586–1607) who in the journey toward the transforming union with God experienced being crowned and adorned by the Lord with bejewelled crowns and necklaces as his spiritual brides. See Teresa de Jesus, *Libro de la Vida*, 33/14; Maria Maddalena de' Pazzi, *I colloqui ii*, 71–79; idem., *I quaranta giorni*. For a thorough explanation of similar mystical experiences see Camilleri, *Union with God*, 175–211.

49. Hurnard, *Hinds' Feet*, 233.

and peace in any situation she found herself in. For quite a long time they stayed at the High Places to learn new lessons from the King himself. Up there they realized that the High Places were only a low place compared with the higher ranges above. Neverending High Places appeared beyond with the result that they could not see the summit. It was only after they pass away in this world that they would be able to enter the other higher places. But they still learned new mysterious matters about the Valley of Humiliation lying below.[50]

They realized that they never could learn everything. Some of the ranges that Grace and Glory observed, below and above them, represented the various aspects of the Truth. But in fact, these ranges taken together represented one whole Truth, and it was beyond their mental capacity to comprehend all this knowledge together. However, she comprehended that Truth based solely on what we read in books can be misleading. Her view was that through personal experience and development we learned more about Truth of love. She remarked that even the Book of Books could be misunderstood if it was separated from the real experiences of daily living, adding that no one could provide a dogmatic perspective about what laid beyond the High Places. In this world one's knowledge through learning was too limited to be able to judge the whole universe. What Grace and Glory suggested was that in the limited time of human existence the only practical way was to remain in communion with the Shepherd.

> She began to understand quite clearly that truth cannot be understood from books alone or by any written words, but only by personal growth and development in understanding, and that things written even in the Book of Books can be astonishingly misunderstood while one still lives on the low levels of spiritual experiences and on the wrong side of the grave on the mountains.[51]

On these High Places, Grace and Glory had a conversation with the Shepherd about her journey. Together they pondered on the lessons of Love that she learned during her ascent, beginning with the first lesson, which was Acceptance-with-Joy. Grace and Glory had accepted with joy what the Shepherd permitted to happen. This was not only through her promise but also through her will on the various altars she built. The

50. Ibid., 235.
51. Ibid., 236–37.

second lesson of love was Bearing-with-Love. This time Grace and Glory had to renounce her doubts and the difficult situations of the journey, particularly the bullying of her Fearings. She learned to forgive without harbouring any ill will toward others. The lesson she learned was that through forgiveness goodness might arise from the evil she faced:

> Therefore I begin to think, my Lord, you purposely allow us to be brought into contact with bad and evil things that you want changed. Perhaps that is the very reason why we are here in this world, where sin and sorrow and suffering and evil abound, so that we may let you teach us so to react to them, that out of them we can create lovely qualities to live forever. That is the only really satisfactory way of dealing with evil, not simply to binding it so that it cannot work harm, but whenever possible overcoming it with good.[52]

In the end, Grace and Glory learned that the Shepherd truly loved her. He did not base his love on how she appeared or how strong she was. The Shepherd loved her unconditionally. This brought her to the third lesson of love:

> I learned that you, my Lord, never regarded me as I actually was, lame and weak and crooked and cowardly. You saw me as I would be when you had done what you promised and had brought me to the High Places, when it could be truly said, "There is none that walks with such queenly ease, nor with such grace, as she."[53]

The Shepherd reminded her about what might occur if she remained near him; to be able to accept and bear everything. Never would she be crippled again, but could leap everywhere close to his Truth and Love. He shared with her the secret of the High Places:

> Accept and bear and obey the Law of Love, and, nothing will be able to cripple your hinds' feet or to separate you from me. This is the secret of the High Places, Grace and Glory, it is the lovely and perfect law of the whole universe. It is this that makes the radiant joy of the Heavenly Places.[54]

At a later stage, Grace and Glory was looking at the sheepfold, at her friends and at her family in the Valley of Humiliation living in misery.

52. Ibid., 242.
53. Ibid., 241.
54. Ibid., 243.

Tears streamed down her face as she appreciated how much they suffered. No longer was she angry with her relatives, but she desired to assist with and alleviate their sufferings. But now she knew that their difficult situation had to be tackled with compassion, and not with despicable thoughts. Her only wish was to change their lives and save them.[55]

Grace and Glory asked the King for advice. She greatly desired to see them free, but mostly she wished to share the joys of the High Places with them. The Shepherd also wished that they were closer to him. The Shepherd asked if she was willing to be his voice and to spread the Good News to them. Grace and Glory instantly acceded to his request. She was ready to proceed to their abode and to share the Good News. However she realized that alone she could not manage to save them. Hence she requested the King to guide and teach her how to proceed. She appreciated the fact that in their misery and morbid context they were more prepared to risk and trust the Shepherd. The best time to convince them was when they were in their most difficult moment in their life and nothing could alleviate their suffering. Like her they would have recourse to the Shepherd knowing that nothing really sustained their liberty and love.

In a determined way they all rose to the occasion like the streams pouring down the heights. They dedicated themselves to the sharing of the Good News with others. They wanted to spread the message of happiness and peace of the High Place. Grace and Glory uttered, "for He loves each one of us as though there were only one to love."[56] The Shepherd leaped down and they followed him. This was the end of Much-Afraid's journey which led her to become Grace and Glory. But it was a new start for Grace and Glory in disseminating what she experienced with others.

55. Ibid., 247.
56. Ibid., 254.

Chapter 2

A Reflection of Hannah's Life

AN INTERTEXUAL ANALYSIS OF
HINDS' FEET ON HIGH PLACES

LIKE OTHER NARRATIVES, *Hinds' Feet on High Places* was designed from many elements which the author synthesized together in a logical and coherent way. In this narrative the author's life stood out. In fact, some scenes in the allegory resembled Hannah's experiences. Through this fictitious narrative Hannah tried to pass on her spiritual and theological messages. However, Hannah did not only compose this narrative to share her messages but also wrote theological books and autobiographies to share, reveal, and propose her spirituality. These other narratives provided the wider picture through which Hannah's allegorical narrative could be understood and interpreted. Thus, this chapter deals with sections of her other publications which appear to be related with the *Hinds' Feet* allegory. In perusing these other publications the themes of this allegorical narrative can be deduced.

HANNAH'S TORMENT AT THE VALLEY OF HUMILIATION

Hannah's personality and difficulties in her teens at Colchester are represented in the character, problems, and circumstances of Much-Afraid prior to her journey to the *High Places*. In fact, Hannah's distressed lifestyle is figuratively presented in Much-Afraid, a name which refers to Hannah's perception on herself.[1] Much-Afraid had two physical limitations, a crooked mouth and limp feet. The easiest association with Much-Afraid's crooked mouth is Hannah's stammering problem. In *Hearing Heart*, her first publication and autobiography, she narrates the following unpleasant experience:

> Until I was nineteen, I never went into a shop alone, nor on to a bus or train, or anywhere where I would be obliged to speak. As a child, when we were playing in the garden alone and I was natural and unselfconscious, I could often say whole sentences, but if spoken to or asked a question, the ghastly struggles began at once. I simply hated people, the unfeeling ones, and even the kind ones who looked away and were horribly sorry and embarrassed. At school I suffered torments and appeared a perfect fool, always saying I didn't know the answers to questions because I couldn't get the answer out. . . . I was set apart from my own kind, and it is perhaps difficult for any normal person to realise how I loathed human beings.[2]

On account of her stammering problem Hannah felt humiliated. This kept her away from the public and made her dislike relationships.[3] In the case of Much-Afraid her problem did not only limit her communication but also impinged on her attitude. The same applied to Hannah. The stammer induced her to feel like a "miserable, morbid, self-centered person who never felt love for anyone, shut up to my [her] own torment."[4] This torment hindered Hannah from living an ordinary life, as confirmed when she uttered these words: "The first nineteen years of my life can be symbolized by the period during which the Children of Israel suffered bondage in Egypt at the hands of Pharaoh's cruel taskmasters."[5] Hannah was also dominated by fears which influenced her moods and behaviour,

---

1. "It is not surprising that the well-read Hannah chose the name of John Bunyan's character in *Pilgrim's Progress* Much-Afraid as the inspiration and title character of her own stories" (Anders, *Story of Hannah Hurnard*, 27).

2. See Hurnard, *Hearing Heart*, 11.

3. "Hannah's playmates consisted of her siblings and children of other wealthy families who visited her home or whose homes she visited. Rarely comfortable in social situations, she always felt like a misfit in the company of other children her age, mostly because of her verbal handicap" (Anders, *Story of Hannah Hurnard*, 6).

4. See Hurnard, *Hearing Heart*, 11.

5. See Hurnard, *Thou Shalt Remember*, 5.

ranging from fear of darkness, terror of heights, terror of crowds to horror of death. On observing how different she is from others, Hannah felt afflicted and reluctant to socialise. Metaphorically, these fears caused her to "limp" like Much-Afraid.[6]

One reads that Much-Afraid's physical defects in walking had an adverse effect on her service to the Shepherd who symbolized Jesus. However, Much-Afraid's service to the Shepherd reflected Hannah's faith and Christian upbringing. At the age of eleven Hannah abided to her Christian religion, but she kept feeling unhappy and doubtful. Although she was encouraged by her family to believe she still perceived the faith as meaningless. For Hannah, "the Bible remained the dullest and deadliest book in the world and going to services the worst kind of hateful boredom."[7] In Much-Afraid's story one does not note her crises to believe, but one reads that in the Valley of Humiliation she was sorrowful and her limping hampered her work. One concludes that Much-Afraid's limping movements expressed metaphorically two problems for Hannah: her struggle to develop one's gifts and character to the fullest and to starve to believe in God.[8]

In the allegory Hannah laid out the main cause of her morbid way of living, metaphorically expressed in Much-Afraid's anguish from the Fearings. These represented two elements. On one hand, the Fearings stood for Pride, Bitterness, Spiteful, and Craven Fear, while on the other hand, they were her Relatives denoting Much-Afraid's kinship to them. The cause of Hannah's unhappiness was related to her fearful and discouraging emotions. Only her escape from the Fearings might change her mood to no longer feel so miserably. Her strong emotional longing was to be positive and closer to God. Although Hannah in her autobiography expressed her dislike toward her family's strict Puritan lifestyle, she appeared to attribute her problems to the way she reacted to them. The more she gave in to bitterness, pride, spite, and gloom, the more she misunderstood her

6. See Hurnard, *Hearing Heart*, 11; idem, *Thou Shalt Remember*, 6, 9.

7. See Hurnard, *Hearing Heart*, 11; one notes that Hannah has failed to form "a disposition of shared trust and loyalty to (or through) the family's faith ethos" (Fowler, *Stages of Faith*, 17).

8. "Feeling far from God was not *just* 'something missing' in her life. It was a gaping hole—a state of torment in which she lived daily, much like the Jews while in bondage to the Egyptians. Constantly during these early years, she felt lonely, afflicted, and despairing" (Anders, *Story of Hannah Hurnard*, 6).

faith and lifestyle.[9] Hence, Much-Afraid's narrative was centred on her capacity to deal with the Fearings. Being the basis of her spirituality, this escapism was endorsed by the Shepherd. As long as Hannah succeeded in suppressing the negative feelings, she would be upbeat and in a position to leap mountains. This belief was highlighted later in the allegory when Much-Afraid, transformed into Grace and Glory, wished to deliver others from their misery by eradicating their negative feelings.[10]

Prior to the beginning of her journey, she narrated how the Fearings attacked Much-Afraid. At first Craven Fear bullied her, and later the relatives intruded into her house.[11] In both cases Much-Afraid ended up being bruised, tormented, exhausted, powerless, and humiliated. Hannah narrated these episodes to explain how the negative emotions took the upper hand. Instead of handling these pessimistic emotions constructively, she allowed them to take the upper hand, resulting in sufferings, which in turn led to a heightened morbid and miserable lifestyle. In these circumstances Hannah attributed her lack of faith to her tormented feelings and to her lack of skill to counter them. In the following abstract one could draw a parallel between Much-Afraid and Hannah:

> Morning after morning I awoke feeling that I simply could not face another day. I longed for the courage to commit suicide. Thus I grew more and more morbid and tormented and shut up to myself, unable to think of anything but my own unspeakable wretchedness. There were still times, when I was alone with Nature, and with animals (who loved me and didn't ask questions or try to make me talk), when I felt almost happy. But they were only brief respites from acute wretchedness.[12]

The opposite characters between the Fearings and the Shepherd were evident. Hannah comprehended that these nagging feelings contributed to her decline in faith in Jesus. However, her answer was to suppress these feelings. As long she was not cynical she would be closer to the Shepherd. As Much-Afraid "never learned to resist or ignore their threats" so was Hannah in her lack of skills to control these torments. Faced by this situation, Much-Afraid called at the Shepherd where "she felt sure he would

---

9. See Hurnard, *Hearing Heart*, 34.

10. See Hurnard, *Hinds' Feet*, 244–54.

11. Ibid., 32, 38.

12. See Hurnard, *Hearing Heart*, 11–12.

help her and not permit her relatives to kidnap her."[13] In this context, the Valley of Humiliation represented the state of fear and humiliation of Hannah. One confirms what John Wood stated about *Hinds' Feet on High Places*, that "the secret of its [the story's] influence lies in that fact that it's a story of a fear-ridden girl setting off for the High Places in company with her much-loved Shepherd, is in fact the romance of Hannah's own personal pilgrimage."[14]

Much-Afraid's handicaps and intimidations by the Fearings compelled her to seek help from other sources. In her case she was assisted by the Shepherd. This happened also to Hannah. Her stammering problem and the fears caused her to avoid contact with others. The anguish was so intense that it crushed her. She yearned to be peaceful and free. In spite of her circumstances, Hannah also was helped by the Shepherd. A change came over Hannah when she attended the Keswick convention with her father. Being among people and in her inner confusion she experienced another crisis, leading her to cry and kneel at her bedroom. On seeing her father acceding to the request to let his children go to the missionary services, anxiety and anguish dominated Hannah again. In her father she perceived a kind of inner freedom which she lacked. One concludes that she was a slave to her way of thinking. In the depths of her despair and misery she cried out aloud like Much-Afraid to her Shepherd, "O God, if there is a God anywhere, You must make Yourself real to me. If You exist and are really what these people describe You to be, You can't leave me like this."[15] Representing Hannah as Much-Afraid, one may conclude that she reached directly the Valley of Loss; a place of terror and dread to sacrifice her stammer.[16]

> Here I was . . . the place of sacrifice. The place where I must yield myself utterly to One who would, somehow, in some agonizing way, put me to the horror of crucifixion. And the THOUGHT came to me vividly and clearly, in a dreadful flash of mental

---

13. See Hurnard, *Hinds' Feet*, 19.

14. Wood, *Hannah Hurnard*, 9; "With adoring wonder, as I look back over the years, I clearly see that it was those early experiences of living in bondage to fear and then finding my prison door thrown open and the way into freedom revealed that allowed me the privilege of writing a book entitled *Hinds' Feet on High Places*" (Hurnard, *Thou Shalt Remember*, 11).

15. See Hurnard, *Hearing Heart*, 15; Wood, *Hannah Hurnard*, 39.

16. See Hurnard, *Hinds' Feet*, 170–80.

enlightenment, "What this unknown God is going to demand before He makes Himself real, is that I yield Him my stammering tongue, and agree to be His witness and messenger."[17]

However, even though in her heart and mind she was aware of what had to be done she struggled to surrender her will.[18] In *Hinds' Feet on High Places* one notes that Much-Afraid also struggled to give way to her will. In fact, Much-Afraid had to struggle to accept moments which called for sacrifices. It could be stated that the scene at the Valley of Humiliation portrayed Hannah's dilemma in her bedroom when she was assailed by doubts and morbid thoughts. One notes a connection between what Hannah recounted in *Hearing Heart* and what Much-Afraid saw at the Valley of Loss.

> And I cried out in almost frenzied dismay, "No I can't do that. I would rather go straight to Hell. If I can't know God any other way, I won't know Him at all." And then the dreadful realisation swept over me, "But it's as though I am in Hell already. Oh, I need him. I need Him. No one else can help me."[19]

> During that awful moment or two it seemed to Much-Afraid that she was actually looking into an abyss of horror, into an existence in which there was no Shepherd to follow or to trust or to love—no Shepherd at all, nothing but her own horrible self. Even after, it seemed that she had looked straight down into Hell. At the end of that moment Much-Afraid shrieked—there is no other word for it. "Shepherd," she shrieked, "Shepherd! Shepherd! Help me! Where are you? Don't leave me!"[20]

Although Hannah offered her suffering due to her stammering problem to Jesus she was terrorized by his image. To her, Jesus was the one who demanded sacrifice, and who constrained everyone to carry the cross. As a result, this sacrifice would hurt her and deprive her of the

17. See Hurnard, *Hearing Heart*, 17; "The Altar—THE PLACE OF SACRIFCE! Ah, that was it! A thrill of terror went through me. For these words suddenly gripped my mind with a pang of agony. Yes, here it was—the thing I had always subconsciously dreaded. Christians said that Christ Himself was the sacrifice, the substitute for our sacrifices. But in that bitter moment I knew that there was no escape from the truth. I too, like the men of old, must lay on the altar a sacrifice."

18. See Anders, *Story of Hannah Hurnard*, 14.

19. See Hurnard, *Hearing Heart*, 17.

20. See Hurnard, *Hinds' Feet*, 172.

things she obtained throughout her life. Reaching this rash conclusion she uttered that she preferred to go to hell than to yield herself.

> Even as a child, in the strictly Evangelical home in which I had been brought up, this thought had always haunted me. If only one could find God without Jesus Christ. God Himself sometimes sounded like a kind and good Father, but JESUS WAS TERRIBLE. He said, "No one can come to the Father but by Me," and that all that come to Him must take up the Cross as He did, putting self to death in order to be able to follow Him, and that they must sell *all* that they have, or they cannot be His disciples.[21]

In retrospect, Much-Afraid is picturing Hannah in the Valley of Loss, which is "as low as the Valley of Humiliation itself."[22] Much-Afraid is aware that the Valleys correspond to hell. Her image of Jesus contrasts to that of Hannah's. While Much-Afraid considers the image of the Shepherd as a lover, Hannah has a different view. In fact, Hannah's fears made her renounce the sacrifice, while her spirit confirmed her damnation to hell. On realising her situation, she dedicated herself entirely to Christ. She built her first altar, which was the greatest and last altar of Much-Afraid. In the chapter entitled the "Grave on the Mountains," Much-Afraid proceeded to the altar and she gave in herself to the Shepherd.[23]

> O God, if there is a God, if you will make yourself real to me, I will yield my stammering mouth. . . . And at that moment I became as sure that He stood there beside me as if I had seen Him with my eyes. I felt nothing I saw nothing. But into my lonely, dark, tormented heart, there flooded, like a burst of sunlight, the realisation which has never left me all these twenty-six years. Jesus is real. He is here. He loves me, even me. After all, he loves ME, and has come to tell me that he wants me, that He will use me, even with my stammering, use me whom nobody else wants, who am so handicapped that I supposed I could never become of use to anyone. He wants me. He is real. . . . HE IS REAL: HE IS HERE: HE LOVES ME: He actually loves me. I am perfectly safe.[24]

After the sacrifice Hannah experienced the graces of the High Places. Although she was weak and had a stammering mouth she realised

---

21. See Hurnard, *The Hearing Heart,* 16.
22. See Hurnard, *Hinds' Feet,* 171.
23. Ibid., 208.
24. See Hurnard, *Hearing Heart,* 15.

that God always loved her. She used Much-Afraid to express this reward and realisation. On reaching the High Places Much-Afraid learned the following lesson:

> That you, my Lord, never regarded me as I actually was, lame and weak and crooked and cowardly. You saw me as I would be when you had done what you promised and had brought me to the High Places.... You always treated me with the same love and graciousness as wretched little Much-Afraid.[25]

A TRANSFORMED ATTITUDE

When she experienced God's love, Hannah was transformed. Now she was perceiving life completely different. "The old fettering and tormenting husk had cracked and fallen off. In one sense an utterly new girl was kneeling on the floor, a girl who for the first time in her life felt joy, felt secure, felt able to laugh, could have clapped her hands and dance for sheer ecstasy of heart."[26] Hannah's ecstasy corresponded with Much-Afraid's great happiness in chapter 17, when Much-Afraid enjoyed the healing streams. At this moment, Hannah assumed a new name depicting her new attitude toward life. She started to look at life with an expanding outlook for the grace and glory of God. One is reminded when Much-Afraid was given a new name, which was Grace and Glory.[27] In a nutshell, through her utter surrender to Jesus, she had been "transplanted from a tiny flowerpot, into sunny, richly fertilized flowerbed."[28] Hannah realised that even though she was exhorted to believe in creeds and dogma, faith

---

25. See Hurnard, *Hinds' Feet*, 241.

26. See Hurnard, *Hearing Heart*, 18.

27. "Her parents had always told her that her name, *Hannah*, meant 'God's grace'! This second assurance meant to her that whenever anyone would call her by name, she would immediately be reminded of these words and know, again, that in her own human weakness, God's grace would at last fine its home" (Anders, *Story of Hannah Hurnard*, 27); "THE FOUNDATIONAL TRUTH I learned in the School of Earth Experience is this: we are spiritual beings who can never find true satisfaction and happiness except by recovering our lost God-consciousness and uniting our wills with his" (Hurnard, *Thou Shalt Remember*, 5).

28. See Hurnard, *Hearing Heart*, 19.

made the difference in her life. Only through faith Hannah was able to make contact with God and save her from bondage.[29]

During her first journey Hannah reached the High Places. But now the second journey led her back at the Valley of Humiliation. Even though she experienced God's love and had a new transforming outlook toward life, her fearful nature was still present.[30] On descending from the High Places she had to face the reality of life, but with a new vocation. She now lived closer to Christ, and like Much-Afraid, she was now at the service of the Shepherd. One notes that the allegorical journey of Much-Afraid manifested two dimensions in Hannah's life. One was her inner feelings and thoughts, and the other one her desperate way of living. Both these elements interacted and influenced Hannah's allegorical narrative. Moreover, during this new journey Hannah, like Much-Afraid, had a new instrument to guide her. This was the seed of Love, which could be correlated with the "Hearing Heart." The Hearing Heart was Hannah's essential vital force which she defined it as an "utter dependence upon Him and willingness to respond and obey."[31] Indeed, the seed of Love implanted in Much-Afraid taught her new lessons by the Shepherd and also gave her that push to trust him.[32] This was similar to Hannah's other text *Hearing Heart*.

> THE GREAT PRINCIPLE of the "Hearing Heart" is that we "BE-COME AS LITTLE CHILDREN," utterly dependent and always ready to obey. We have to learn to obey His guidance in small personal matters, before we can receive and understand more of His will and purpose.[33]

As stated previously, after Keswick, Hannah proceeded to Ridgelands Bible College and later enrolled with the Friends Evangelistic Band.[34] Hannah realized that the journey was going to be tough. Indeed, "looking shrinkingly towards the future, it seemed to me [her] that, handicapped

29. See Hurnard, *Thou Shalt Remember*, 12.

30. See Anders, *Story of Hannah Hurnard*, 15.

31. See Hurnard, *Hearing Heart*, 12.

32. See Hurnard, *Hinds' Feet*, 27, 49, 83, 126, 204.

33. "'Hearing Heart' depends upon an utter willingness to obey, the whole time, in tiny details as well as big ones. In Hebrew an 'obedient heart' is the same as a 'hearing heart.' If one hears the Voice of God, it should mean obedience, and if one obeys one will hear" (Hurnard, *Hearing Heart*, 85).

34. See Hurnard, *Hearing Heart*, 35; Wood, *Hannah Hurnard*, 45.

as I [she] was, every step of the way before me [her] must cost pain and tears and humiliation."[35] Leaving Keswick she still treasured the lessons of the Convention. Apart her intimate encounter with Jesus, she also cherished advices imparted by the speakers.

> They warned us to keep separate from everything which would tend to draw us back into the old life of unbelief. They urged us to witness to others, for if we were not willing to share in this way, we would soon find that we had nothing left to share, and everything would become unreal to us again. And they underlined the immense importance of daily, thoughtful, playful study of the Bible.[36]

Although she was ready and enthusiastic to accept advice, Hannah's life was undoubtedly full of dilemmas as well as surprises. While Hannah was occupied with her mission of teaching and sharing the Good News, she followed a path which led her to be immersed in Jesus's love. Through her allegorical narrative Hannah described the journey metaphorically. This journey of Much-Afraid's beginning at the Valley and ending in Kingdom of Love had frequent diversions and hardships due to the terrain and the inclement weather. In addition, she had to face the relentless attacks from the Fearings. Confronted by these difficulties Much-Afraid had to discern the situations and to act accordingly, always in a loving way. One notes that all these problems, diversions, and struggles were inspired by Hannah's experiences in life, which imbued her with an understanding of God's salvation. These elements were represented symbolically in the allegory. Among the diversions which Hannah had to face was when she received a calling to proceed to Palestine and evangelize to the Jews. Unfortunately, her work connected with the Friends Evangelistic Band in the United Kingdom was wound up. In Ireland she asked for direction from God. During her prayers she narrated the following:

> A thought came in my mind, as though naturally following the train of previous thoughts, but with a clarity and significance which seemed a personal challenge. "Hannah, would you be willing to identify yourself with the Jewish People in the same way, if I asked you to?"[37]

---

35. See Hurnard, *Hearing Heart*, 22.

36. See ibid., 23; Anders, *Story of Hannah Hurnard*, 21.

37. See Hurnard, *Hearing Heart*, 49.

However, she viewed this calling as a contradiction. Because of her previous experiences in Palestine she loathed the Jews and thus refused to travel over there. Considering the fact that she was not proficient in languages and that she disliked the Jews, she could not understand God's call.[38] To make things worse, Jews considered women unable to communicate God's Word. Even friends from the Band were sceptical about her new call as she lacked the necessary training to work in Haifa. Nevertheless, at the Ireland's Eye she submitted her will and accepted her new calling. On enrolling with the British Jews Society she was accepted to travel to Palestine. To her disappointment she had to wait for four years before permission was granted to evangelize in Palestine. In the meantime, she worked as a stop-gap teacher and nurse, an occupation which distressed her as it did not harmonize with her call. In these circumstances she doubted whether God really spoke to her. Moreover, the work made her weary. Indeed, Hannah became impatient. To complicate matters, the worship services in the mission field differed from her usual services. They were conservative and devoid of initiative for personal prayers. "I found these new Staff Prayer Meetings painfully chilling and repressive."[39] In her book *Standing on High Places*, Isabel Anders states that:

> Mentally she pondered whether or not this was truly the place to which God had been leading her. *If so, where was the glory, or even the grace to endure?* She lamented. When overtaken by the pain of loneliness and near-despair, she commonly dropped onto her bed, still dressed, and simply shocked, feeling as if she would fall through the mattress into an endless abyss. The "lowest place" often seemed too low to bear.[40]

It is to be pointed out that although at long last she was granted permission to visit the Jewish villages to evangelise, she encountered some problems. These problems ranged from lack of transport to lack of companions.[41] However, after several requests she was donated a van

38. Ibid., 50–51; Wood, *Hannah Hurnard*, 55; Anders, *Story of Hannah Hurnard*, 64; Hurnard, *Thou Shalt Remember*, 65.

39. See Hurnard, *Hearing Heart*, 57; Wood, *Hannah Hurnard*, 74; Hurnard, *Watchmen on the Walls*, 11; Anders, *Story of Hannah Hurnard*, 76–86; Hurnard, *Thou Shalt Remember*, 69.

40. Anders, *Story of Hannah Hurnard*, 82.

41. See Hurnard, *Wayfarer in the Land*, 21; Hurnard, *Thou Shalt Remember*, 84.

from England. Also some companions from the mission field joined her in her quest to undertake evangelistic work.

> I had not even been specially praying that the door would open for me to launch out into evangelistic work, although when I had first arrived on the mission field it had been with high hopes that I would speedily be able to move out into the villages to undertake direct evangelistic work. But for four years that door had not opened, and shortage of staff, combined with my own inexperience and lack of necessary language, had barred the way, and it still seemed as though I never would be freed for the special work for which I had felt called.[42]

All these delays to fulfil her calling inspired Hannah to narrate in a splendid way Much-Afraid's descent to the Desert, the loneliness she endured at the Shores of Loneliness and her walk on the Old Sea Wall. Finally she deemed all these delays as blessings from God who taught her to trust him, to control her impatience and to learn her new skills to be used later. Like Much-Afraid, she considered all this diversions as contradictions, but soon realized that they were postponements and preparations. In *Hearing Heart* she recounts:

> In actual fact this was all part of the new discipline and development which the Lord saw I must now undergo. It was exactly what was needed next. For bubbling, frothing new wine cannot continue to spill and splash over for ever. It must be constrained and confined in some way, or it will never become mellowed and sweetened and made ready for its best use.[43]

Following her lessons at the Desert, the Shores of Loneliness and the Old Sea Wall, Much-Afraid was ready to focus on her journey to the High Places. Now the difficulties were due to the terrain and the path she had to follow. Much-Afraid had to face a Great Precipice Injury and a Forest of Danger and Tribulation. The difficulties Much-Afraid had to endure to climb the precipice and at the forest were all inspired by Hannah's own experience while at Palestine journeying from one village to another. To climb the deep precipice Much-Afraid had to clamber its sides and to pass through narrow paths. In this situation she could have fallen and died. It was the same feeling that Hannah had when she travelled in her van from

42. See Hurnard, *Wayfarer in the Land*, 12.
43. See Hurnard, *Hearing Heart*, 58.

one Arabic or Jewish village to the other on muddy road.[44] During this travelling she had to face dangerous attacks and rebellions.

> Call came in 1936, just at the time when the Arab riots against the Jews, which were to last three years, broke out in their fury. During that time the roads in the country were infested with mines, buses and cars were the targets for snipers, and for nearly three years no civilian cars were allowed on the roads unless they were in military-protected convoys.[45]

Despite the dangers that Much-Afraid had to endure climbing the precipice and confronting the darkness at the Forest of Tribulation, she succeeded in overcoming these hurdles. Hannah's success in reaching all the Arab and Jewish villages around Haifa, proclaiming the Bible, prompted her to prevail over these perils. A few weeks before the British Mandate on Palestine was coming to an end, Hannah together with her companions visited selected villages where she touched the hearts of hundreds who were suffering from the war and conflict between the Jews and Arabs. In *Wayfarer in the Land* she recounted that in all her dangerous traveling she was protected by God. To the surprise of many she was never harmed. Despite her success in her vocation Hannah had to confront another contradiction. Violence and terrorist attacks on British civilians escalated to such an extent that Operation Polly took effect and all the British civilians were repatriated to their country. It was at that time that Hannah experienced the Mist from *Hinds' Feet on High Places*. Back to her country against her will now she was no longer near the Jews and Arabs as she had been called. Hannah saw this episode as yet another contradiction to God's call.[46] In this situation she could not envisage what was required of her, yet she still remained faithful despite being under stress.[47] Her wish was to go back. In fact, when the opportunity arose she accepted against her will to be engaged as a housekeeper.

---

44. See Wood, *Hannah Hurnard*, 84; Hurnard, *Wayfarer in the Land*, 39, 41, 64, 69, 112, 128; Anders, *Story of Hannah Hurnard*, 95, 101.

45. See Hurnard, *Hearing Heart*, 60.

46. "I can never express what those words meant to me. All the promises did indeed seem contradicted and God had not intervened to prevent our being driven forth from our Land of Promise, but He still remained faithful" (Hurnard, *Hearing Heart*, 69; Anders, *Story of Hannah Hurnard*, 121; Hurnard, *Thou Shalt Remember*, 102).

47. See Hurnard, *Hearing Heart*, 71; Wood, *Hannah Hurnard*, 112.

I dropped both the letters with a thrill of horror, and then began to laugh from sheer nervousness. My ever vivid imagination began to function at once, then seemed to shy back appalled from the picture of chaos, shame and confusion which it produced. Instinctively from long habit I began speaking to the Lord and said, "What can have possessed them to suggest such a thing, Lord? How little they know me. I never heard any suggestion so preposterous."[48]

Yet the Hearing Heart, or the seed of Love, kept reminding Hannah about Palestine. Hannah was reluctant to accept this type of work in Palestine, even if she knew that this was God's will. During her prayer she offered her hesitation to God, but eventually she accepted work as a housekeeper in Palestine even though she was in the dark about what was in store.[49] On arriving in Palestine the retired housekeeper taught her what her duties involved. Despite her doubts, she realized that God was behind her becoming a housekeeper. At that time the British mandate in Palestine was about to expire. The Great Floods mentioned in *Hinds' Feet on High Places* were about to take place. On the mandate's termination, war erupted between Jews and Arabs in Palestine. When the conflict was at its height, Hannah was residing in a house in Jerusalem. Both Much-Afraid and Hannah went through similar circumstances. While Much-Afraid found refuge in a cave during the flood, Hannah also took shelter in her small house in Jerusalem during the heavy bombardments.

In her little cave Hannah took all her memories of God symbolized in pebbles and remained steadfast in her faith. Despite the adverse circumstances she remained in Jerusalem assisting the wounded. In *Watchmen on the Wall* Hannah narrated her experience when she was in the Jewish Quarter in Jerusalem at a time when the violence in the city escalated. The following is an abstract of her experiences:

Suddenly a series of tremendous explosions occurred, apparently exactly overhead. I felt paralysed with fright as they crashed down one after the other. I dared not run downstairs; it felt as though the roof must fall at any moment. Finally they ceased and I moved towards the stairs with my legs shaking. I heard Ruth calling me. "Hannah, come down, come down quickly. Some has been hit. I am afraid it is Yehuda." For a moment I could not move, and then went to the front door. Ruth stood there wringing her hands. Just

48. See Hurnard, *Hearing Heart*, 75.
49. See Hurnard, *Hearing Heart*, 76; Anders, *Story of Hannah Hurnard*, 122.

inside our gate, nearly on the doorstep, lay Yehuda, facing us, resting on one hand, blood spattered all over him. I shall never forget the stunned look of horror on his face, and the pitiful beseeching way he looked at us without a word.[50]

Alas, I find myself very nervous now that the shelling has started again, and seems to be getting nearer. By supper time on the very first evening the mortars had started. They were not very close, but the feeling that at any moment they might get our range again was horrid. We all seem to find it worse than we did before.[51]

THE FEARINGS' CONSTANT ATTACKS

Besides the obstacles and difficulties that Hannah encountered in Palestine, she had to face another problem regarding her inner spirit and emotions which did not put her at ease. Like Much-Afraid, Hannah had to confront the many attacks from the Fearings. Pride, Resentment, Bitterness, and Self-pity, tried every possible way to hinder her in her journey. These four feelings represented some of the manifested feelings that intervened in her execution of her work and as a consequence influenced her decisions. Who tried to control Hannah was no longer Craven Fear but a number of feelings which impinged on her clear judgement and enhanced her doubts.[52] These feelings assailed her up to the end of her mission in Palestine even if she became more spiritual and enhanced her knowledge about God. The worst feeling which subtly tormented Hannah

---

50. See Hurnard, *Watchmen on the Walls*, 134.

51. Ibid., 158.

52. "Craven Fear still tormented Hannah after her renewal at Keswick. There is an episode in Hannah's life when she decided to go to Ridgeland Bible College. In one of her classes Hannah had to give a talk to her fellow students as part of her training. She recounts: 'But when I first made the appalling discovery that in one week's time I must address the assembled staff and students, I felt that it was grotesquely impossible and that I ought never to have come. I cringed with fear and then rushed to my cubicle, and going to the drawer, took out my purse, with the intention of taking a ticket for home at once'" (Hurnard, *Hearing Heart*, 27). Hannah also shares with us how she was able to fight her fears. She came to see fears as scarecrows, "If I am wise I TOO SHALL TREAT THE SCARECROW AS THOUGHT WERE A DINNER BELL. . . . Every giant in the way which makes me feel like a grasshopper is only a scarecrow beckoning me to God's richest blessings" (Hurnard, *Hearing Heart*, 33; Wood, *Hannah Hurnard*, 44; Anders, *Story of Hannah Hurnard*, 32).

from the beginning of her journey was Pride. Hannah realised pride had an impact on her relations with others with the result that her friends passed negative comments on her and judged her personality. She was saddened by their reaction. During her prayers in the presence of Jesus she realised that it was true that pride was part of her ministry.[53] Although she now experienced God's love, she concluded that her comportment remained the same. Faced with this situation she decided to change her behaviour and put aside her pride, which was due to her imagination and daydreaming.[54]

> And then, suddenly I saw it. Because the act of "burning incense" before self in this way, namely enthroning self in the center of the stage of the imagination, is inescapably certain to puff one up with an inflated feeling of superiority. In my daydreams I was always the heroine-a gracious, charming, gifted, yet humble heroine whom others delighted to honour. And there it was, as clear as crystal before me, that was where the proud, superior Miss Hurnard evolved from.[55]

While she was sharing with the non-Christian believers the Good News about Love toward others she sensed a contradiction. Hannah realised that she wasn't living up to the love of Christ toward her friends at the mission field. What she wished was to love in all circumstances and situations acting according to his law. In *Kingdom of Love* Hannah realized what a Christian attitude involved. She had to love at all costs in all situations, but how would she respond to and act in a situation which went against God's will? In this state she was confused, and Bitterness and Resentment assailed her.

> The sensations and feelings of resentment and bitterness would come sweeping over me like an irresistible wave, and while they lasted each time, there I was, battered and hating myself, yet clinging to the Lord, telling Him I detested these feelings, that I trusted Him to save me from them, insisting that He enable me to meet

53. "For, pride, is the greatest cause of unbelief and unreality in spiritual things, and looking foolish is one of the ways by which 'we take up the cross' and crucify our pride" (Hurnard, *Hearing Heart*, 45; Anders, *Story of Hannah Hurnard*, 66, 88; Hurnard, *Kingdom of Love*, 34; Hurnard, *Thou Shalt Remember*, 43, 47, 81).

54. See Wood, *Hannah Hurnard*, 51; Anders, *Story of Hannah Hurnard*, 38; *Kingdom of Love*, 60.

55. See Hurnard, *Kingdom of Love*, 59.

them triumphantly, and as more than victory over them; even reminding Him again and again that His name was Jesus, Savior, and
that He was called Jesus because He promised to save His people
from their sins, and that if He could not save wicked, hateful me
in this unexpected and apparently overwhelming situation, and
make me victorious in love, He was not worthy of His name, and
that I would never be able to preach again to anyone that He was
a Savior who could save the uttermost. That if He didn't prove His
power now I was lost.[56]

However, Hannah imparted to us the way she adopted to reach a bal-
ance in her problems. In Much-Afraid's story building altars and offering
the struggles was a common occurrence. Being confused and in a state of
fear Hannah had recourse to God for his counsel in her quiet time. One
notes that the altars that Much-Afraid built symbolized Hannah's quiet
time and her method of prayer.[57] Hannah learned that "sacrifice is the
ecstacy of giving the best we have to the one we love the most."[58] Quiet
time is Hurnard's method of prayer. Waking up early in order to pray was
Hannah's way to keep close to God's will. Hannah learned this method of
prayer through her family and through her education at the Ridgeland
Bible College, a method adopted by the Quakers. According to Hannah
these quiet times were absolutely necessary as during this time she was
able to communicate with her Shepherd and present to him her problems
including her desires. At the same time she stood waiting for his advice.

We were urged to rise at least three quarters of an hour earlier
every morning, in order to MEET THE LORD AND LISTEN TO
HIM. This was stressed as the most important essential of all, and
we were told that nearly all the people acknowledged that they
had slipped back into indifference of unreality in spiritual things,
confessed that it began with neglect of the Daily Quiet Time, and

56. Ibid., 70.

57. See Hurnard, *Thou Shalt Remember*, 19–20: "So I began a completely new kind
of life, learning to build daily altars of surrender to God's will and receiving his enabling
grace to lay down my self-inspired longings. Looking back over the long years of memory, my life seems to be one bright vista of early morning hours of communion with the
Lord, and nothing else seems important in comparison. So life has become more and
more a yearning to spend time in the heavenly places with him and his loved ones, even
while still here on earth in a mortal physical body" (24).

58. Ibid., 46.

failure to give the Lord an opportunity to speak to them alone and to train them in hearing His voice.[59]

> There have been times since then when I have been tempted to think He asked too much, more than I could give, when for a few moments submission or obedience have looked too costly to be possible. Only for a moment or two, than God, for during those moments I have had an appalling glimpse into that awful existence where He is not known and not obeyed, which is Hell. Then he has gently brought me back to this glorious truth: that sacrifice is indeed the ECSTASY of giving the best we have to THE ONE WE LOVE MOST. When that is the experience of the heart, sorrow and disappointment and heartache become sweeter than the greatest natural happiness.[60]

For her reading the Bible was like reading letters of love by Jesus. In fact, she was very close to Jesus during these quiet times.[61] As these quiet times touched Hannah's heart and imparted to her new lessons of love, she immediately put them down in her journals. Her journals represented the pebbles that Much-Afraid picked up throughout her journey. These pebbles symbolized important memories and reminded her of new lessons and acts of grace from Jesus.[62] Through these journals we gain more knowledge about the two flowers of love that Much-Afraid discovered during her journey. These two flowers, Acceptance-with-Joy and Bearing-with-Love, taught Much-Afraid the lessons to accept and bear whatever God's will presents. She summarized these two flowers of love in the following abstract:

> I find that when the Lord calls to some act of obedience which looks absurd, or doubtful, or even wrong it is necessary to take the first step in obedience without paying any attention to doubts or fears. But when we have begun to obey, then we must go to the Lord with all our questionings and the criticism of others, to ask if we are still to proceed or if there is anything we should modify or change. Always begin to obey, and after every new step ask if it is

---

59. Ibid., 23, 39.

60. Ibid., 47.

61. Ibid., 24. See also Gregory the Great, *Epistle to Theodorus*, 156.

62. Hurnard, *Thou Shalt Remember*, 86.

His will that we should keep going forward. He is faithful, and will check us if we have not really understood His mind.[63]

These two lessons were mentioned in her other books, particularly in her book entitled *Kingdom of Love*. The lesson Acceptance-with-Joy taught Hannah was to accept everything that God called her to do, while the one Bearing-with-Love taught her was to accept all the problems faced while fulfilling God's will.[64] These problems included those provoked by others, but she had to accept and forgive the persons involved. Another lesson she endured throughout her journey dealt with the hardships which had to be faced with a positive and trustful outlook in Jesus. In *Kingdom of Love* she referred to these lessons "as it were, a very simple but utterly tremendous alphabet or ABC of love."[65] These two alphabets of Love discovered by Much-Afraid are further explained in Hannah's journal.

> It is through accepting the circumstance that come to us in life that self is crucified. There is no other way. No reckoning of ourselves as dead to sin can avail anything unless we reckon, or accept the fact, that we have no right to resent anything which is done to us, but that our right is to react to everything in a creative way by using it to express and manifest love in some way.[66] The second letter in the alphabet of love is bearing, which in actual fact is the meaning of forgiveness. . . . To bear means to accept any and all wrong that others do to us, any burden they may put upon us, any infringements of our rights, any losses they may cause us. It goes even further than accepting with joy, because it is the very essence of forgiveness. To forgive is to bear in this way anything that another may do to us, and to say as Christ did, "I choose to bear all that you do to me and still love you and long for your salvation, your rescue and release from sin and self. I will bear whatever it may cost me, and I mean to use the creative power of forgiveness to help you all I can."[67]

At that time Hannah's missionary service in Palestine was coming to an end. When the conflict between the Arabs and Jews abated she had

---

63. Ibid., 61

64. Hurnard, *Walking among the Unseen*, 38, 45, 61.

65. Hurnard, *Kingdom of Love*, 64.

66. Ibid., 67.

67. Ibid., 81.

to travel back to England as her father passed away. Sometime later, she spent a holiday in Cyprus. In this country she learned another lesson about love symbolized in Much-Afraid's entry to the Kingdom of Love. In the allegory no title was given to this lesson, but it was symbolically expressed in her entry to the High Places. But the actual name of this lesson was divulged in the book *Kingdom of Love*. She titled it *Creative Love Thinking*. Through creative and positive thoughts all negative feelings are eliminated and suppressed, and one would be living in the realm of the Kingdom of Love.[68]

> But what I had never clearly realized all through the years was that the kingdom of God is within us, and is in actual fact centered in our thought life. What we are there is what we are actually. "As man thinketh in his heart, so is he." And that of course is why none of us can claim to be different or better than other by nature, because of the appalling things which we discover harbored in our thought life, things which we would have thought ourselves incapable of thinking. . . . I just did not realize that the whole secret of loving lies here, in the thought realm.[69]

> If one never allows irritating, annoying, critical or unloving thoughts to remain in the mind a moment, however strongly they may clamor for permission to remain, and if only creative love thinking is the habit of our thought life, nobody will be able to see through us or in us, thoughts that are not there and our whole outward manner will be transformed.[70]

In her exposition she remarked that the best way to deal with negative feelings and sufferings was by countering them with positive thinking, and thus the feelings would be transformed into love.[71] However, a point should be made on the two guides of Much-Afraid, Sorrow and Suffering, who accompanied her during the journey. Thanks to their help she managed to reach the High Places and learn the lessons of Creative Love

---

68. See Hurnard, *Kingdom of Love*, 97; Hurnard, *Thou Shalt Remember*, 123–29.

69. See Hurnard, *Kingdom of Love*, 51.

70. Ibid., 54.

71. "Naturally this inflow of new power becomes greater as we learn to yield more and more to the control of love, and to block every avenue to the waiting floods of destructive thinking. It was particularly in my own prayer life that I began to discover what a complete transformation this new principle of thinking only creative thoughts could produce" (ibid., 98).

Thinking. Hannah saw suffering and sorrow as requirements that one had to face to comply with God's will. By countering the negative thoughts Hannah had to suffer. However her suffering in fulfilling God's will and in controlling her desires brought her closer to Jesus. Eventually this suffering was transformed into Joy and Peace.[72] Hannah had to choose between two options which both led to suffering and sorrow: either to stop following him and to end up in her past misery, or to suffer to fulfil his will and enjoy the fruits of Love.[73] In *Kingdom of Love* she narrated that when she accepted suffering and sorrow to follow Christ, it brought her closer to him. A change came over her and she experienced his love and enjoyed the spiritual gifts. The more she restrained her desires and worries, the more she experienced God's love. Now she realized what Suffering and Sorrow led to: enabling Hannah to confront her future problems in the conviction that she is fulfilling God's will.

> For example, what is real joy, the joy which cannot be taken from us, but sorrow accepted and transformed. What is real peace, but struggle and strife, fear and anxiety overcome. What indeed is real love but self love overcome and transformed into a passion for self-giving. And probably we shall find that every experience of trial, difficulty and suffering, of wrong done to us and accepted and forgiven, all these things will have worked in us some lovely trophy for eternity.[74]

This revelation compelled Much-Afraid to descend the High Places and go back to the Valley to transform the Fearings. In fact, *Mountain of Spices* narrated how all the Fearings at the Valley of Humiliation changed their names to be in harmony with Jesus's love. What brought about this transformation was Grace and Glory, into which Much-Afraid had converted.[75] In this way she could call at their homes and exhort them to submit their problems to the Shepherd. This final episode in *Hinds' Feet*

---

72. See Hurnard, *Hearing Heart*, 30; Hurnard, *Thou Shall Remember*, 32, 50.

73. "His Love had shut me up to these two alternatives, I must either follow Him no matter what He asked me to do, or turn back to the old nightmare existence of being imprisoned in myself" (Hurnard, *Hearing Heart*, 31).

74. See Hurnard, *Kingdom of Love*, 48; "Thus I gradually came to realise that these two handicaps which had so tormented me were, in reality, two special 'love gifts' from the Lord. They were the two sharp nails which nailed me to Him, so that I could never want or dare to go on my own again" (Hurnard, *Hearing Heart*, 31).

75. Hurnard, *Mountain of Spices*.

on High Places is consonant with Hannah's experience in Cyprus, where she learned a new revelation.[76] In Cyprus, she sensed that God was calling her to publish her experiences and her theology. This is represented in Much-Afraid, who on reaching the High Places shared with others the message of grace and glory of God in the hope that others will respond to the Saviour's call.[77]

---

76. Anders, *Story of Hannah Hurnard*, 134.

77. Wood, *Hannah Hurnard*, 126–27; Anders, *Story of Hannah Hurnard*, 141.

Chapter 3

"Thou Art My Heart's One Choice"

Hannah's Use of the Song of Songs

In her theological arguments Hannah often quotes excerpts from the Bible in support of her reasoning. One notes that some verses were so significant to her that they affected her with tender emotions. To her the Bible was indispensable as she deemed it like "love letters" from God.[1] This metaphor on the Bible signifies Hannah's closeness to God, who loves her unconditionally. She regards the Bible not only as a way of understanding God's revelation but also as an intimate encounter with him. As a result, Hannah's behaviour in its moral aspect was influenced by the Bible. In fact, in *Hinds' Feet on High Places* one encounters many quotations and direct and indirect references to the Bible. Through her allegorical narrative she conveys her theological messages inspired by the Bible, particularly those excerpts on which she based her narrative. This chapter deals with the many biblical abstracts and their connections with this narrative. Through the use of intertexuality the biblical interpretative capabilities of Hannah are better comprehended. Moreover, her selections and interpretations of the biblical quotes highlight her spirituality.

During one of the prayer meetings held in Palestine Hannah was eager to know about the significance of Song of Solomon 2:8. An explanation was given by a nurse who stated that "it means there are no obstacles

---

1. See Hurnard, *Hearing Heart*, 24.

which our Savior's love cannot overcome, and that to him, mountains of difficulty are easy as an asphalt road."[2] This exposition touched her heart. Being a sensitive person she pondered on these words and how she could actually put them into practice. In line with a particular biblical line of thought she associated the mountains with her fears and challenges that were blocking her spiritual growth, and remembering how Jesus leapt upon them so easily.[3] Only through his "leaping" on her "mountains" she understood how much he loved her. Moreover, on reading *The Voice of my Beloved!* she expressed more strongly her closeness to Him. He is not only the beloved, but also *my* beloved, denoting her intense love toward him. Moreover, Hannah combined together Song of Solomon 2:8 with Habakkuk 3:19 and Psalm 18:33 and contemplated their significances.

> "The voice of my beloved!
> Look, he comes,
> leaping upon the mountains,
> bounding over the hills." (Song 2:8)
> "GOD, the Lord, is my strength;
> he makes my feet like the feet of a deer,
> and makes me tread upon the heights." (Hab 3:19)
> "He made my feet like the feet of a deer,
> and set me secure on the heights." (Ps 18:33)

One notes that in Habakkuk and in Psalm 18 both the prophet and the psalmist's "feet" are endowed with the "feet of a deer." Thus, one concludes that these "feet" are not only limited to God. Through God's power and grace they were now able to surmount the difficulties they encountered. As an expression of gratitude they cried out glory to him who transformed their feet into that of a deer. Now Hannah drew a distinction between the Beloved who could "leap the hills" without being prompted and the others who could only "leap" if God could permit their "feet" to be like those of a deer. She now realised that if she wished to undergo the same experience of the psalmist and prophet and join them in their praise to God, she had to remain close to God. Only through her intimate

---

2. See Hurnard, *Hinds' Feet*, 9.

3. In the sacred Scriptures, mountains are not only the privileged places of divine revelation but also metaphors of obstacles to be overcome through God's intervention. In Scripture, mountains that stand for pride (Dan 2:35, 45), oppressive power (Jer 51:25), and idolatry (Jer 2:20; 3:23) become the object of God's wrath. See "muntanja" in Leon-Defour, *Temi Biblici*, 478–82.

relationship with God she could overcome her difficulties and traumas in life and could learn the secret of victorious living. This victorious living meant that through prayer she could react to sufferings and tribulations in loving ways. In this way she would resemble the Lord's character. What inspired Hannah to compose this narrative was the Song of Songs, not only because she quoted sections from this biblical book throughout the narrative but also because she viewed the Song of Songs as the song which "expresses the desire implanted in every human heart to be reunited with God himself, and to know perfect and unbroken union with him."[4] Through this unbroken union with the Lord, God taught her lessons to react to her way of living and thus to be able to leap and tread the heights. In fact, the narrative of Much-Afraid is a journey to remain in union with Christ, who teaches her how to handle the difficulties and "mountains of trials" she encounters in her life to reach the High Places. She realised that God was the person who "descended upon her mountains" to deliver her from bondage. Now her desire was to ascend and reach the High Places where "perfect love casts out fear" (1 John 4:18). Hannah mentions 1 John 4:18 twice to describe generally the High Places as a state free from the bondage and torments of fear.

THE SONG OF SONGS

Throughout her allegorical narrative Hannah primarily refers to the Song of Songs. To make clear the messages she wishes to convey one finds various stanzas from the Song of Songs in support of her message. One recalls when Much-Afraid was at the Valley of Humiliation and on asking for counsel from the Shepherd she was invited to proceed to the High Places. Hannah summarised the jubilation of Much-Afraid by quoting from Song 1:1–6. One notes that she was not always accurate in her biblical interpretation but modified it somewhat to blend with the character in her narrative.

> "The Song of Songs," the loveliest song,
> The song of Love the King,
> No joy on earth compares with his,
> But seems a broken thing.
> His Name as ointment is poured forth,

4. Hurnard, *Hinds' Feet*, 10.

And all his lovers sing.
Draw me—I will run after thee,
Thou art my heart's one choice,
Oh, bring me to thy royal house,
To dwell there and rejoice.
There in thy presence, O my King,
To feast and hear thy voice.
Look not upon me with contempt,
Though soiled and marred I be,
The King found me—an outcast thing—
And set his love on me.
I shall be perfected by Love,
Made fair as day to see.

After her first meeting with the Shepherd, Much-Afraid sang this stanza of love on her way back to her house, verses which conveyed feelings of satisfaction and love. Although Much-Afraid tried in many ways to be content in the Valley of Humiliation, it was all in vain; "no joy was on earth." However, after her meeting with the Shepherd she sang this love song as she discovered what she had searched for. The intense desire of Hannah was fulfilled when the Shepherd poured forth the smooth oil of healing and gave her encouraging counsel. Infused with energy by the Shepherd's "ointment," she pleaded with him to take her to his "royal house." For Hannah the royal house and the High Places were synonymous. She wanted to be brought in his royal chambers to experience complete joy, peace, and sumptuous food in his presence and away from the distress at the Valley of Humiliation. On arriving at her house she rested in her bed and sang another section of the Song of Songs and pleaded again with the Shepherd to tell her the place where he took his flock to graze. Her wish was to be part of the flock of the Shepherd who sustains and protects his sheep.

Although Much-Afraid longed to be taken to the High Places, she knew it was premature to enter that place in her current state. She was "soiled" and "marred" due to her stay at the Valley of Humiliation. However, the Shepherd, who was also referred to as King, looked upon her with favour. Through his mercy and love she would be refined and rendered free from impurities. In the case of Much-Afraid this refinement could only occur if she escaped and journeyed with the Shepherd. On waking up the following day she sang another song from the Song of Solomon while making the necessary arrangements for the journey.

Now when the King at table sits,
My spikenard smelleth sweet,
And myrrh and camphire from my store
I pour upon his feet.
My thankful love must be displayed,
He loved and wooed a beggar maid.
Ye daughters of Jerusalem,
I'm black to look upon
As goatskin tents; but also as
The tent of Solomon.
Without, I bear the marks of sin,
But Love's adorning is within.
Despise me not that I am black,
The sun hath burned my face,
My mother's children hated me,
And drove me from my place.
In their vineyards I toiled and wept.
But mine own vineyard have not kept.
I am not fair save to the King,
Though fair my royal dress,
His kingly grace is lavished on
My need and worthlessness.
My blemishes he will not see
But loves the beauty that shall be.
(Song 1:12–15; 5:6)

Much-Afraid was enthusiastic and happy. Grateful toward the Shepherd, she already imaged how she would manifest her appreciation to his kindness. When he would recline at the table she would pour her "spikenard upon his feet" as a gesture of love toward a "beggar maid" as she was. Hannah embodied the "beggar maid." The "beggar maid" represented not only a beggar asking for food that fulfilled her desire but also a maid at his service.[5] One notes that there was a connection between the bride's "blackness" in the Song of Songs and Hannah's sins. However, the Shepherd still loved her and bestowed on her his "kingly grace." The Shepherd saved her from her "worthlessness" and satisfied her "need." But in the case of Much-Afraid this stanza did not yet apply to her as she was still in the Valley of Humiliation. Therefore, Much-Afraid imagined what could

---

5. The word *maid* can be also defined in its archaic sense, meaning she is a virgin open to his grace.

happen once she arrived at the High Places. In fact, on her arrival she confirmed that the King really loved her as he rectified her "blemishes."

In spite of her enthusiasm Much-Afraid was put to the test. While she was preparing for the journey, the Fearings invaded her house. Faced with this situation Hannah cited another abstract from the Song of Songs to depict the scene when the Shepherd called her to start the journey. Trapped in her house she listened to the Shepherd singing the secret song as a sign to join him.

> The Voice of my Beloved!
> Through all my heart it thrills,
> He leaps upon the mountains,
> And skips upon the hills.
> For like a roe or young hart,
> So swift and strong is he,
> He looketh through my window,
> And beckoneth unto me.
> "Rise up, my love, fair one,
> And come away with me,
> Gone are the snows of winter,
> The rains no more we see.
> "The flowers are appearing,
> The little birds all sing,
> The turtle dove is calling,
> Through all the land 'tis spring.
> "The shoots are on the grapevines,
> The figs are on the tree,
> Arise, my love, my fair one,
> And come away with me.
> "Why is my dove still hiding?
> When all things else rejoice,
> Oh, let me see thee, fair one,
> Oh, let me hear thy voice."
> (Song 2:8–14)

The Shepherd arrived near her house "leaping upon the mountains." He looked through her window, calling and instructing her to follow him. This was the beginning of the journey, which meant escape from the "snows of winter" and from the "rains" of the valley. For Much-Afraid now "spring" approached. She began the journey leading to the High Places where she would learn how to overcome her temporal problems and to be relieved of the humiliation she had to face. On seeing the Shepherd pass through the window, Coward covered her face with his hands. In these circumstances she lacked the courage to answer to the call and act in accordance with the Shepherd's command. Fears dominated Much-Afraid. Now she failed to acknowledge the merit of the journey. When the Shepherd perceives Much-Afraid's failure to respond to his invitation, he humbly asks, "Why is my dove still hiding?" While the Shepherd was disappointed, he still desired to see her. The situation was now reversed. At this particular moment, Much-Afraid was not yearning to see the King, but the King himself wished to meet her. Knowing that he had no right to intrude into her house, the Shepherd respected Much-Afraid's free will to use her discretion to his call. On receiving no response from Much-Afraid, the Shepherd walked away.

As fear impinged on her reaction Much-Afraid remained confined to her house bruised by the aftermath of the negative feelings. When the Fearings departed from her house she realised what had happened. She rejected his call of love. When the Shepherd left she was alone shivering with cold. Much-Afraid was now a lost soul not knowing what she could do. In these circumstances, Hannah resorted to another section of the Song of Songs which inspired and spurred Much-Afraid to seek the Shepherd in the dark night. In this section Hannah refered to another shepherdess who "just like herself, had failed to respond to the call of love and then found, too late, that Love had gone away."[6]

> By night on my bed I sought him,
> He whom my soul loveth so.
> I sought—but I could not find him,
> And now I will rise and go—
> Out in the streets of the city,
> And out on the broad highway;
> For he whom my soul so loveth,
> Hath left me and gone away.
> (Song 3:1–3)

On thinking about her refusal to the Shepherd's call Much-Afraid was not at ease. During the night she slipped out of bed and went out to look for him in the dark streets to confirm if he truly left her behind and started the journey without her. The thorn of love which the Shepherd implanted in her heart did not set her at rest. What urged her to find him

6. See Hurnard, *Hinds' Feet*, 50.

was the state of distress she found herself in. To make matters worse, the Shepherd's watchmen informed her that he had already left to the High Places. For a moment, Much-Afraid lost courage but she was determined to find him. In fact, she found him at the trysting-place. At this place the verse of Song of Songs 3:4 occurred to her:

> And then—in the dawn I saw him,
> He whom my heart loveth so.
> I found him, held him and told him
> I never could let him go.

It was dawn and the sun shone through the Shepherd. Much-Afraid fell at his feet crying and supplicating with him to take her with him. It never crossed the Shepherd's mind to leave without her. Knowing Much-Afraid well he waited for her until she decided to join him. He took her by the hand and kept walking until they met with her companions. During this walk the Shepherd taught her the splendid lesson to love everyone. Much-Afraid was amazed with this new lesson. In that environment she sang another set of lyrics found in the Song of Songs.

> I am the Rose of Sharon,
> A wild anemone.
> As lily 'mong the thorn trees
> So is my love to me.
> An apple tree 'mong wild trees
> My Love is in my sight,
> I sit down in his shadow,
> His fruit is my delight.
> He brought me to his palace,
> And to the banquet hall,
> To share with me his greatness,
> I, who am least of all.
> Oh, give me help and comfort,
> For I am sick with shame,
> Unfit to be his consort,
> Unfit to bear his Name.
> I charge you, O ye daughters,
> Ye roes among the trees,
> Stir not my sleeping loved one,
> To love me e'er he please.
> (Song 2:1–4, 7)

Comparing herself to a flower amongst the thorn trees she felt different tasting the "apple" of love. Nevertheless, she was delighted to learn new matters about life. Sitting "down in his shadow" she liked to gain knowledge. Much-Afraid felt diminutive and shameful when she saw the Shepherd acting in a kind manner toward her. He was imparting new lessons to a little creature. Knowing that she trusted him, he brought her to his "palace" where he shared with her new teachings and showed her compassion and love. Although Much-Afraid was frightened by the guides that he selected for her, it was only when she accepted the Shepherd's choice of guides that he called her for the first time, "thou art all fair, my love; there is no spot in thee" (Song 4:7). In fact, Hannah quoted from the Song of Songs to accentuate her way of representing her relationship with God. Moreover, she also quoted from the Song of Songs to foretell events in the narrative. A case in point was when Much-Afraid stood in front of the desert. At first she didn't trust the Shepherd's decision. It was only after she sacrificed her anxiety that she risked trusting God. The Shepherd lightened her burden by singing to her Song of Songs 4:12–17 to predict what will happen to her.

> A garden closed art thou, my love,
> Where none thy fruits can taste,
> A spring shut up, a fountain sealed,
> An orchard run to waste.
> Awake, north wind! And come, thou south!
> Blow on my garden fair,
> That all the spices may flow out
> As perfume on the air.

The Shepherd compares her to a "closed garden," a "sealed spring," and an "orchard" full of fruit going to waste. She resembles a "closed garden" and the Shepherd walks in it. He knows her completely, and unconditionally appreciates her soul's beauty. Moreover, her soul is exclusively to the Lord, and it is only he who will transform her into an "open garden" which will pour out and will share her fragrance to the world. He will help her gain the necessary skills to know herself. But, it is through her journey to the desert that she will learn novel matters about herself. She will be transformed into a better tool at the hands of the Shepherd. When Much-Afraid accepted the Shepherd's decision to descend into the desert he called her beautiful. During Much-Afraid's walk in the lifeless desert, Hannah used biblical characters from the Old Testament. Much-Afraid observed these characters and made her way into the pyramids. Hannah noted a logical historical sequence in God's revelation which is recorded in the Holy Bible. Hannah sought to depict the desert as a lifeless place or darkness[7] where God teaches the human soul to depend on Him. It was a place or state where Hannah lost all the possessions of the soul.[8] The Shepherd kept reassuring her by uttering to her, "Fear not, Much-Afraid, to go down into Egypt; for I will there make of thee a great nation; I will go down with thee into Egypt; and I will also surely bring thee up again."[9] Hannah quoted from Genesis 46:3–4 to communicate to the reader the way she spelled out the Holy Scriptures. Although these words were uttered to Joseph by God, Hannah put them in practice to her situation. She contended that the historical events in the Bible could be applied to one's daily life as a way God speaks to the soul. Hannah perceived various stages of her life which resembled historical events in the Bible. In her spiritual journey she realised that she had to experience spiritual deserts where God would teach her new lessons. While in Egypt, Much-Afraid observed three types of work mentioned in the Bible. Moreover, Hannah employed other abstracts which were not from the Song of Songs to show how the "north wind and south wind" would blow over Much-Afraid's "closed garden," out of which emanated her perfumes to be enjoyed by others.

What she first observed in the Egyptian pyramid was how grains were crushed and ground up to be made into powder for bread making. During the whole process the Shepherd said:

7. Hannah interprets the darkness that fell on Abraham in Gen 15:12 as a way how God communicates with his people, "All of My servants on their way to the High Places have had to make this detour through the desert. It is called 'The furnace of Egypt, and an horror of great darkness' (Gen. 15:12, 17). Here they have learned many things which otherwise they would have known nothing about" (ibid., 85).

8. "Abraham was the first of My servants to come this way, and this pyramid was hoary with age when he first looked upon it. Then came Joseph, with tears and anguish of heart, and looked upon it too and learned the lesson of the furnace of fire. Since that time an endless succession of My people have come this way. They came to learn the secret of royalty, and now you are here, Much-Afraid. You, too, are in the line of succession. It is a great privilege, and if you will, you also may learn the lesson of the furnace and of the great darkness just as surely as did those before you. Those who come down to the furnace go on their way afterwards as royal men and women, princes and princesses of the Royal Line" (ibid., 86).

9. Ibid., 87.

"See . . . how various are the methods used for grinding the different varieties of grain, according to their special use and purpose." Then He quoted, "Dill is not threshed with a threshing instrument, neither is a cart wheel turned about upon the cummin; but dill is beaten out with a staff, and the cummin with a rod. Bread corn is bruised, but no one crushes it forever; neither is it broken with the wheel of a cart nor bruised with horsemen driving over it."[10]

The Shepherd quoted from Isaiah 28:27–28. Hannah represented herself like a grain which was being threshed by the Lord. Different methods of "threshing" were employed to every type of grain. Though the process was painful, it did not pulverize the grain. Hannah regarded this type of work as God's wish to unfetter her from certain bonds to be purified.[11] Metaphorically, God intended to "thresh" Hannah in order to partake in Christ's bread. The second task which Much-Afraid observed at the pyramid was the making of clay into beautiful forms, a process which involved both creative skill and workmanship. At this moment the Shepherd uttered to Much-Afraid:

"In Egypt, too, I fashion My fairest and finest vessels and bring forth instruments for My work, according as I see fit." Then He smiled and added, "Cannot I do with you, Much-Afraid, as this potter? Behold, as the clay is in the hand of the potter so are you in My hand."[12]

Hannah gave a brief account of Jeremiah 18 in one of the paragraphs of the narrative. The second task followed the separation process of grain from its husks. Hannah interpreted these tasks in this way: after being separated from what impeded her from being a tool in Jesus's hands, she could be moulded into an unblemished figure. Symbolized as clay she received a request from the Shepherd whether she was willing to be the clay he would mould. This underscored her opinion that most of the works she observed were inspired by God to attain her spiritual maturity. But Jesus never imposed his will on her; she was free to accept or reject his invitations. The Shepherd quickly reassured her that even though she accepted to be transformed and to partake of the bread of life, she had to be bruised. However, when her transformation was complete the Shepherd

10. Ibid., 88.
11. See Hurnard, *Winged Life*, 40, 45.
12. See Hurnard, *Hinds' Feet*, 89.

promised her that he would bestow jewels on her. One finds this promise in the following words: "My rarest and choicest jewels and My finest gold are those who have been refined in the furnace of Egypt."[13] This promise was made after Much-Afraid observed the third and last task in the pyramid where gold was being smelted and refined in the furnace.

> O thou afflicted, tossed with tempest, and not comforted, behold, I will lay thy stones with fair colors, and lay thy foundations with sapphires. And I will make thy windows of agates, and thy gates of carbuncles, and all thy borders of pleasant stones (Isa. 54:11).

The Shepherd quoted Isaiah 54:11 to assure her that even if the transformation might cause pain and difficulties he would take care of her. In the meantime he promised to reward her with "jewels" for complying with his suggestions. Now her "foundations" would be laid with sapphires which might imply that now she was imbued with unfailing wisdom. Even her "stones" would be rendered attractive. This might denote that her body would regain a fresh vitality. Her eyes would also be transformed into "jewels" to discern better the word of God as she glimpsed through the "windows" and "gates" of her heart and mind. Lastly, her "borders" would be provided with "pleasant stones" so wherever she went she would be protected and be a witness of the Shepherd's grace. One concludes that if Much-Afraid complied with the Shepherd's ways of refining his pilgrims before entering the High Places, she would be rendered splendid. The three tasks in question led Much-Afraid to the flower of Acceptance-with-Joy. At this point she proceeded with her journey, which was not always smooth. During her transformation she sometimes had to undergo hardships but she recalled the tasks in Egypt and the rewards she would receive in return. In fact, when she was at the Shores of Loneliness where she had to face solitude and the attacks of her fears she quotes from the Bible to remind herself to remain steadfast in the Shepherd's teachings:[14] "When He hath tried me, I shall come forth as gold. Weeping may endure for a night, but joy cometh in the morning" (Job 23:10; Ps 30:5). It was only after her gradual transformation that she began to confront her problems otherwise. Now Much-Afraid was able to proceed to the foot of the mountains which led to the High Places. As she was willing to act on his teachings, the Shepherd allowed her to journey

13. Ibid., 90.
14. Ibid., 96, 101.

directly to his Kingdom. At the appropriate time he uttered these words: "I have come to bring you a message," said the Shepherd. "You are to be ready, Much-Afraid, for something new. This is the message, 'Now shalt thou see what I will do (Exod 6:1).'" [15]

One notes that Hannah resort to Exodus 6:1 to narrate what was in store in Much-Afraid's journey. One reads in the narrative that Much-Afraid faced other difficulties in the course of the journey, such as the precipices, the mists, and floods. Yet the Shepherd imbued Much-Afraid's heart with hope and trust. Although Much-Afraid was afraid of these perils, she continued with her journey to find the next flower: Bearing-with-Love. Once she trusted in his judgements and endured the difficulties she had to face during the journey, the Shepherd sang again to her another song from the Canticles:

> Thou art all fair, my dearest love,
> There is no spot in thee.
> Come with me to the heights above,
> Yet fairer visions see.
> Up to the mount of Myrrh and thence
> Across the hills of Frankincense,
> To where the dawn's clear innocence
> Bids all the shadows flee.
> Come with me, O my fairest dear,
> With me to Lebanon,
> Look from the peaks of grim Shenir,
> Amana and Hermon.
> The lions have their dens up there—
> The leopards prowl the glens up there,
> But from the top the view is clear
> Of land yet to be won.
> (Song 4:7–8)

In this stanza the Shepherd lauded Much-Afraid for climbing the Great Precipices. Although he called her again "fair" because she no longer carried "no spot" of sin, the Shepherd expected much more of Much-Afraid. He urged her to strive to attain a higher perfection in her quest for holiness. The more she mounted the more she might recover her lost "innocence" due to sin. The Shepherd knew that the journey would pose new difficulties, yet he reassured her of his presence as she faced the

---

15. Ibid., 115.

"leopards and lions."[16] Though the Shepherd was physically absent during the mist, she was not spiritually alone. As she faced the darkness and the opposition from the Fearings she sang a Shepherd's song to prevent the negative feelings and thoughts from impinging on her faith.

> How lovely and how nimble are thy feet,
> O prince's daughter!
> They flash and sparkle and can run more fleet
> Than running water.
> On all the mountains there is no gazelle,
> No roe or hind,
> Can overtake thee nor can leap as well—
> But lag behind.
> (Song 7:1)

In this scene Much-Afraid is experiencing uncertainties. When Hannah was subject to similar moments to doubt she instructs the readers how she learned to overcome these negative feelings and thoughts. In this state she mentally cited quotes from the Bible. In doing so, she discovered a vitality which helped her to conquer any immoral desires. She also resorted to this technique in her brisk walks. In fact, while she was walking toward the High Places she was more "nimble" than those who journeyed to that place. At a later stage the Shepherd took her to the place of anointment. Hannah quotes Isaiah 6:9 when the Shepherd purged her of her sins.[17] He prepared her for the final part of the journey and uttered the verses from Revelation 3:8–12.

> Thou hast a little strength and hast kept My word, and hast not denied My name. . . . Behold I will make thine enemies to come and worship before thy feet, and to know that I have loved thee. Behold, I come quickly: Hold fast that which thou hast, that no man take thy crown, and she that overcometh will I make a pillar in the temple of My God, and she shall go no more out: and I will write upon her the name of My God. . . . I will write upon her My new name.[18]

16. Ibid., 141.

17. "Then the King told her to kneel and with a pair of golden tongs brought a piece of burning coal from off the altar. Touching her with it He said, 'Lo! this hath touched thy lips; and thine iniquity is taken away, and thy sin purged' (Isa. 6:7)" (ibid., 192).

18. She omits a part from this quote, which is, "Look, I have set before you an open door, which no one is able to shut," however in her biographies she uses this quote to go and evangelise the villages before the mandate came to an end. It seems she removes it in

Although, the innate character of Much-Afraid was fragile and un-reliable, she remained faithful to the Shepherd. When she encountered difficulties she was gripped by anxiety, but she never denied him. Thus, the "King" shall "crown" her and bring her "enemies before her feet." She would enter his chambers and becomes a "pillar" in his temple. More-over, her new name would honour her. The Shepherd encouraged her not to give up. Indeed, the Shepherd was aware of the future events. Much-Afraid found herself in a situation where she had to be the next sacrifice on the altar where her corrupt love had to be eradicated. After this trans-formation Hannah quotes several passages from the Bible to manifest the degree of faith Much-Afraid had attained. Despite being scared Much-Afraid cried out: "Though He slay me, yet will I trust in Him" (Job 13:15), and again: "My Lord, behold me—here I am, in the place Thou didst send me to—doing the thing Thou didst tell me to do, for where Thou diest, will I die, and there will I be buried; the Lord do so to me, and more also, if aught but death part Thee and me (Ruth 1:17)."[19]

This is the most important point in Much-Afraid's spiritual journey. Her progressive transformation has reached a state in her faith which makes her fully rely on the Shepherd's wisdom and grace. Obeying his commandments Much-Afraid is ready to die for his glory; even if death itself is hindering her from union with him, she is prepared to face it. This entire reliance led her to the High Places where she joined her "King." Now she changed into true Love in all its aspects. Her natural feelings and affections, which were an obstacle to experiencing the true love of the Shepherd, were eradicated. At the High Places she received her new name, Grace and Glory,[20] while her guides were transformed into Peace and Joy, which later were the handmaidens of Grace and Glory.[21] At the High Places, Grace and Glory learned more intimately about God's love. The reason she had received hinds' feet was she learned to readily ac-

---

the allegory because it doesn't make sense in the process of the story (ibid., 194).

19. Ibid., 213.

20. "I will write upon her a new name, the name of her God. The Lord God is a sun and shield: the Lord will give grace and glory: no good thing will He withhold from them that walk uprightly" (Ps. 84:11) and "This is your new name," He declared. "From henceforth you are Grace and Glory" (ibid., 226).

21. "The King's daughter is all glorious within. She shall be brought unto the King in clothing of wrought gold, in raiment of needlework. The virgins, her companions that follow her, shall be brought unto thee. With gladness and rejoicing shall they be brought: they shall enter into the King's palace (Ps. 45:10–15)" (ibid., 230).

cept and bear God's will. She comprehended that only through creative thoughts in love could her sorrow and suffering be transformed into joy and peace. Full of awe toward the wonders of God's wisdom, Grace and Glory also reached a High Place in her heart from where she sang the last song:

Set me as a seal upon thine heart
Thou Love more strong than death
That I may feel through every part
Thy burning, fiery breath.
And then like wax held in the flame,
May take the imprint of thy Name.
Set me a seal upon thine arm,
Thou Love that bursts the grave,
Thy coals of fire can never harm,
But only purge and save.
Thou jealous Love, thou burning Flame,
Oh, burn out all unlike thy Name.
The floods can never drown thy Love,
Nor weaken thy desire,
The rains may deluge from above
But never quench thy fire.
Make soft my heart in thy strong flame,
To take the imprint of thy Name.
(Song 8:6)

To portray her profound love for Jesus, Grace and Glory sang this song. Her only intense desire was to be deeply immersed in his true love and be united intimately with him in heart and soul, as symbolized in the word "seal." In being so intimately united, separation was extremely difficult. She wanted to be "a seal upon his heart" to enjoy eternal peace and love. She also wanted to be a "seal upon his arm" so that she participates in the salvation of others to be delivered from sin and its consequences. Above all, she wanted to be close to him so that when temptations, problems, and suffering besotted her they did not undermine her faith and love in him. At this point, Grace and Glory was ready to descend the High Places to encourage others to start the journey leading to the Kingdom of Love and meet the King of Love.

HANNAH AND THE SPIRITUAL SENSE

What made Hannah consider the Song of Solomon in such an intimate and profound manner was the allegorical interpretation of a verse which was stated to her by a nurse in Palestine: "The voice of my beloved! Look, he comes, leaping upon the mountains, bounding over the hills (Song 2:8)."[22] This interpretive approach impelled Hannah to narrate and appreciate the sacred Scriptures in a new manner.[23] Now she is perceiving the implicit meaning of the Bible. Although this also happened to Hannah when she was at Cheswick while reading a passage from the Old Testament book of Ezekiel, it was only now that she became familiar with the hidden meaning of the sacred Scriptures. In fact, she ardently utilized this new way of interpretation in her allegorical narrative after her missionary service in Palestine.

Although in her autobiographies and theological books Hannah did not divulge this new technique of hermeneutics, one notes that Hannah exploited Sacred Scripture to support her own ideas and principles through citations and extracts. Unfortunately, it appears that information about how Hannah analysed the Holy Scriptures is not available. However through her style of writing she imparts to the reader vital moral lessons. It is to be pointed out that this genre of writing was pioneered by Origen of Alexandria (185–254 AD). In her lack of knowledge about the biblical spiritual sense underlying the literal meaning of sacred Scripture as discovered by Origen,[24] Hannah appears to be influenced by such hermeneutics. By focusing on the Song of Solomon Hannah has drawn on the prominent spiritual sense which Origen has extensively discussed in his treatises.[25]

One notes that in our times Origen is still deemed as the pioneer in the thought and depth of mystical formation.[26] In fact, many scholars peruse his commentary on the Song of Songs as it is the first distinguished production of Christian mysticism. He was convinced that the Holy Spirit is the one behind the mysteries underlying the letter of the law and that

22. Ibid., 9.

23. Ibid.

24. See Origen, *Song of Songs* 8; see also "The Doctrine of Scriptural Senses" in Quasten, *Patrology*, 2:92–93.

25. See de Lubac, *History and Spirit*, 159.

26. See King, *Origen on the Song of Songs*, 3.

it was God's wish that these mysteries be concealed to those that are not initiated in the faith so as to protect what is sacred from being profaned. According to Wisdom 7:21 he reached the conclusion that the Bible covers two meanings, one which is manifest and the other one which is veiled. Origen comprehended that the apparent meaning was not opposed to the spiritual. On the contrary, the apparent meaning is the foundation on which one can delve deeper into the hidden concepts of God, and as a result, live through meaning which is finer than the letter. R. P. Lawson affirms about Origen:

> And he doubtless shows by this that each of the manifest thing is to be related to one of those that are hidden; that is to say, all things visible have some invisible likeness and pattern. Since, then, it is impossible for a man living in the flesh to know anything of matters hidden and invisible unless he has apprehended some images and likeness thereto from among things visible, I think that He who made all things in wisdom so created all the species of visible things upon earth, that He placed in them some teaching and knowledge of things invisible and heavenly, whereby the human mind might mount to spiritual understanding and seek the grounds of things in heaven; so that taught by God's wisdom it might say: *The things that are hid and that are manifest have I learned.*[27]

Following this conviction Origen begins to look at existence in a new perspective. By linking the visible object to the invisible wisdom of God, everything could be appreciated fuller through the Divine Wisdom who edifies the soul. According to Origen this enlightenment, which is blurred to the human being, is unveiled through the grace of the Holy Spirit. This conclusion also applies to the Divine Scriptures. In fact, Origen connects this revelation with the mystery of the Incarnation of God. For Origen, this is the cosmological-theology key which is derived from Song of Songs.[28]

Employing the invisible and visible factor, Origen examines the sacred Scriptures. The visible corresponds to the body of the text, which is the obvious and historical, whereas the spirit is the "element of heaven of

27. See Origen, *Song of Songs*, 220.

28. Ibid., 9; "Per lui [Origene], si puo stabilire un'equazione costante tra I termini: intelligibile, spirituale, invisibile, incorporeo, celeste. Tutto l'ordine visibile, materiale, terrestre, riceva allora il ruolo di essere similitudine dell'invisibile e di condurci al divino grazie alla sua contemplazione" (Charles, *Il Dio dei mistici*, 77).

which it offers an image."[29] Origen asserts that as the Logos has been incarnated in God-Man, so the incarnation of the "Pneuma" in Holy Scripture is divine-human.[30] The human element is that which the senses can comprehend while reading the texts, while the divine element is the Holy Spirit which exposes the spiritual wisdom. Origen applies this exegesis to the Song of Songs. He concludes that while the literal sense of the Song of Solomon is a drama involving a bride and a bridegroom, the spiritual insight of the song is about the "mystical union" between the Bridegroom (Christ) and His bride (Church and Soul).[31]

One notes that Hannah was influenced by the Song of Songs in the spiritual sense. This shows that her narrative was much related with Origen's study. She perceived the Song of Songs as a spiritual drama involving her soul with Christ and manifesting Jesus's love toward the individual soul. In her exposition and in that of Origen's, one finds many parallels. As a case in point, Origen's description of the "wound of love" corresponds with Hannah's "thorn of love."[32] By this "wound of love" Origen has meant that "the soul is moved by heavenly love and longing when, having clearly beheld the beauty and the fairness of the Word of God, it falls deeply in love with His loveliness and received from the Word Himself a certain dart and *wound of love.*"[33]

The "wound of love" is the apprehensive emotion which is instilled in an individual on coming into contact with the glory of God. After a lot of soul searching and lack of peace, the heart is "wounded" by the intense desire to unite with God. Only through direct access to Jesus the soul is fulfilled. This is the main reason why Much-Afraid endures the pilgrimage; a journey through which every person gradually in union with Christ is enlightened prior to be made perfect. As a result, the holy nuptial-marriage with God is consolidated. This journey is accomplished only through His grace: "He leads her on and on from a knowledge of self,

29. See Origen, *Song of Songs*, 9.

30. Ibid., 9, 154; King, *Origen on the Song of Songs*, 29, 45–51.

31. See Origen, *Song of Songs*, 21; King, *Origen on the Song of Songs*, 5.

32. Origen, *Song of Songs*, 29; "Where have You hidden Yourself, And abandoned me in my groaning, O my Beloved? You have fled like the hart, Having wounded me. I ran after You, crying; but You were one" (John of the Cross, *Spiritual Canticle*, 1).

33. Origen, *Song of Songs* 29.

to the struggle against sin, to practice of asceticism to the mystical ascent, until at last she is admitted to the mystical union with Him."[34]

This progressive bond in Christ is highlighted in Pauline theology, especially when discussing the difference between the inner and outer man: "so we do not lose heart. Even though our outer nature is wasting away, our inner nature is being renewed day by day" (2 Cor 4: 16). Saint Paul predicts that while the external man's lust and passions are put aside, the inner man is nourished by charity and hope. Origen warns that the Song of Songs is a song of love unsuitable for those who interiorly remain like "childish-man." The Song describes the spiritual journey of those who through faith allow their "inner man" to discover new ways of growing in the divine mystical union through love (Eph 4:13).[35]

Although Hannah's examination of the Song of Solomon is akin to Origen's, it lacks the profound aspect of the nuptial-marriage of Christ with the Church. Despite the fact that Hannah speaks of the difficult situations regarding the lack of union of the Christian churches, she doesn't apply the Song of Songs to this problem as Origen does.[36] This shows that Hannah lacks the profound ecclesiology of mainstream Christianity regarding the reality of the universal Church, echoed also in Origen's *Commentary on the Song of Songs*.

In using the Song of Songs to manifest the qualitative characteristics of the *ecclesia ex gentibus* (represented in the Song by what he calls "the woman of the Gentiles"),[37] Origen demonstrates how those who obtain superior gifts and love from the Holy Spirit are in a state where they receive a lot because they are children of this church and therefore are in a better situation to recognize the love of Christ. Therefore, when Origen observes the "blackness" of the bride he doesn't merely comprehend the marks of sins, as Hannah did, but he further perceives that this "blackness" is due to the bride's lack of enlightenment before encountering the Love of Christ.[38] Notwithstanding the fact the children of the *ecclesia ex gentibus* were not part of the Chosen People, who received the Lord's progressive revelation by the prophets of old, they were still treasured

34. Origen, *Song of Songs* 15.

35. Ibid., 157, 170.

36. Hurnard, *Kingdom of Love*, 107.

37. Origen, *Song of Songs* 12, 13, 94, 102.

38. Origen, *Song of Songs* 91, 99.

by the Lord since they were also created in the image of God; through Him her *illud primum* had been restored.[39] When Origen comments on the "vineyards that the Bride did not keep," he was not limiting his comment to the sins that the soul commits because she doesn't observe the commandments but regards the "vineyards" as the tradition of the Law and the Prophets which the soul forsakes because the beloved Himself is directly in communion with her.[40] In Origen's sight the soul considers Christ who passed over the prior knowledge which was given from His "companions" (prophets), and now He is the ultimate wish. At this stage, one expects Origen to emphasize that in interpreting the Song of Songs, one should not only not separate the soul from God but also the soul's relationship with God's from the ecclesiological dimension.[41] R. P. Lawson shows how Origen makes it clear that they ought to be always taken together:

> We should speak of the parallelism of the relationship between the Divine Word and the Church and between the Word and the Soul. But more than a parallel is involved; at the base of it is the intimate relationship of being between the Church and the Individual soul. As has already been suggested, the Church is identical with the *coestus omnium sanctorum* [as if all were one people]. Origen states clearly, simply, "We are the Church"—*Ecclesia . . . nos sumus* (*Hom.* 2.3).[42]

In Origen's point of view, the verse which stimulated Hannah to compose this narrative had a deeper spiritual connotation. "The voice of my beloved! Look, he comes, leaping upon the mountains, bounding over the hills" (Song 2:8). The beloved is not simply "leaping" on the struggles that souls face in this world, but for Origen the beloved also "leaps" on what has been proclaimed about Him. He is willing to attract toward Him the soul who has been detached from God's radiance and embraces her

---

39. Origen, *Song of Songs* 92, 104, 107.

40. Origen, *Song of Songs* 115–18.

41. "Thus Origen's exegesis does not confer on the Bride a single and fixed value. Instead, she becomes an ever-appreciating commodity in the economy of salvation, being neither exclusively the individual soul nor exclusively the perfect Church. The Bride is, on Origen's reading, both soul and Church-individual and collective person- conceived in the light of a continuous, ordered, voluntary progress towards the perfection that will be fully unveiled only at the end of ages" (King, *Origen on the Song of Songs*, 15).

42. Origen, *Song of Songs* 15.

in his "bosom."[43] Through his Incarnation He gives Himself to everyone who believes in Him. Hence, Jesus is always compassionate to the soul who pleads for harmony and joy. On the other hand, neither the Law nor the Prophets can quench the true thirst of the human heart. It is only He who gratifies the true needs of the heart.[44] Indeed, the Beloved is "the way, and the truth, and the life. No one comes to the Father except through me [him]" (John 14:6).

43. Origen, *Song of Songs* 64.
44. Origen, *Song of Songs* 73.

Chapter 4

Hannah's Spirituality

A PAINFUL STRUGGLE FOR INTEGRITY

HANNAH'S MYSTICAL CONTRIBUTIONS

THE GREATEST SPIRITUAL MERIT that *Hinds' Feet on High Places* offers to the readers is the concept of transformation. In the narrative Much-Afraid and Grace and Glory are in complete contrast. While they refer to the same individual, they are unlike in their spiritual maturity. Hannah uses these archetypes to illustrate her transformed persona from Much-Afraid to Grace and Glory.[1] Any reader is intrigued by these names, in particular with that of Much-Afraid. To some extent fear dominates everyone in some way or other, and thus one would subconsciously identify oneself with the character of Much-Afraid.[2] This is not something novel by Hannah. John Bunyan (1628–88) exercises a similar allegorical style in *The Pilgrim's Progress*.[3]

---

1. See Hurnard, *Walking among the Unseen*, 11–12.

2. "Over time, he [Jung] realized that when he managed to translate his emotions into images, he was inwardly calmed and reassured. He came to see that his task was to find the images that are concealed in the emotions. . . . He used a number of expressive techniques to give symbolic form to his experience" (Chodorow, *Jung*, 2).

3. Bunyan, *Pilgrim's Progress*.

On perusing this narrative the readers would regard themselves as sharing the feelings manifested by Much-Afraid. Much-Afraid's relation with the Shepherd, her circumstances, the songs she cites from the Song of Solomon, and her decisions have an impact on the reader's mind. Therefore, her gradual transformation makes the readers ponder their current conditions.[4]

One has to bear in mind the point of departure in any transformation. When the current situation of an individual is far from happy one seeks to make it different through a material psychological and spiritual transformation, always in the hope to be content and self-satisfied.[5] In fact, this occurred to Hannah when she yearned for happiness. This is the starting point of one's own experience. Like Much-Afraid the reader also endures difficulties which bring about pain to achieve the desired goals. Hannah's desire was that her life would have had a significance and be perfected. One notes that the readers relate to Much-Afraid in that they wish to be content and be positive in heart and soul like her. If their goal is not attained, one concludes that this is due to some stumbling block. In her allegorical narrative Hannah indicates the elements which impinged on her transformation. The main cause was the Fearings, who caused her a lot of anguish. The other elements, which had an adverse impact on her transformation, were feelings of pessimism, fear, gloom, and spite. Readers easily comprehend these feelings, but they can include others which impinge negatively on their character. Hence, her quest for freedom and happiness was a primary goal. One notes that when these "negative" feelings intensify and are suppressed they become a prison that confines the soul in desolation and anguish. Hannah describes this state in the symbol of the Valley of Humiliation.[6]

4. Jung remind us that active imagination is a natural, inborn process. Although it can be taught, it is not so much a technique as it is an inner necessity (Chodorow, *Jung*, 3); "Jung also makes a distinction between active imagination and passive imagination. An active fantasy may be evoked when we turn our attention towards the unconscious with an attitude of expectation. With passive attitude, fantasy is not invoked, rather it drifts around unnoticed, or it erupts into consciousness uninvited" (Chodorow, *Jung*, 6; Burke, "Healing Power," 14).

5. Downey, *Understanding Christian Spirituality*, 14.

6. "Many people feel mentally imprisoned: imprisoned by drugs and alcohol, by their part or childhood, by poverty or loneliness, by their genes. It is odd that in this free society so many people feel themselves to be constrained. Even wealthy and successful people often feel trapped. We have become free only to find that it is often an empty liberty"

In these circumstances, Hannah attempted to cope with these adverse elements at the Valley of Humiliation. She wasn't passive, but the counsel she received from Mrs. Valiant was not adequate to fulfil her desire and mitigate her suffering. Mrs. Valiant expresses the advice given to her by relatives and friends. This might also apply to the readers. However, the help given is inadequate to quench the longings or sufferings. Jesus, in the tale, is represented by Hannah as the real antidote; Jesus is the one who counteracts evil. In her allegory the impression is given that she began to believe in Jesus not after receiving exhortations but only after she experienced His love.[7] Hannah concludes that when one experiences Jesus in mind and spirit, one will get to know and believe in Him.[8] In knowing Him Hannah lived through his grace. Readers who have experienced the grace of God confirm Hannah's conviction: "The human being discovers his true essence only if God finds access into his life and influences his Spirit."[9] In the allegory Hannah symbolizes Jesus's grace as fruits at the High Places. When she experienced Jesus's love she was blessed and enlightened. Hannah concurs with Saint Paul's pronouncement: "Christ Jesus had made me his own" (Phil 3:12). One notes that she eventually regarded life as pleasant, holistic, and divine. Moreover, God's blessing meant that she would spiritually "multiply" as God had prom-

---

(Radcliffe, *What Is the Point?* 31). "The failure to renounce the inordinate attachment produces an imprisonment of the soul" (Beck, *Soul Provider*, 18).

7. Gula, *Call to Holiness*, 25–27. We see in Hannah Hurnard the importance of experiencing God rather than believing in a set of beliefs like a creed without any experience of God in one's own life. We see this emphasis originating from her background knowledge as a Quaker. Indeed Quakers emphasis this experience of God more importantly from a belief in a set of rules (Durham, *Spirit of the Quakers*, 40). In the allegory Hannah writes that no one can provide a dogmatic perspective about what lay beyond the High Places (Hurnard, *Hinds' Feet*, 235). This can be related with the symbol of "ladder" that Saint John of the Cross uses to describe one of the features of the *dark contemplation*: "Speaking now somewhat more substantially and properly of this ladder of secret contemplation, we shall observe that the principal characteristic of contemplation, on account of which it is here called a ladder, is that it is the science of love. This, as we have said, is an infused and loving knowledge of God, which enlightens the soul and at the same time enkindles it with love, until it is raised up step by step, even unto God its Creator" (John of the Cross, *Dark Night*, 5); see also "Negative Theology," in Hopkins, *Nicholas of Cusa*, 86; Zammit, *Men's Call*, 46–47.

8. "A spiritual experience stands at the beginning of a spiritual journey" (Gutierrez, *We Drink from Our Own Wells*, 35).

9. "L'uomo trova la sua vera essenza solo se Dio entra nella sua vita e lo pervade del suo Spirito" (Grun, *Il coraggio di trasformarsi*, 9).

ised to Abraham when He blessed him and summoned him to journey with Him (Gen 12:2). On becoming aware of God's love she realised that the entire universe was governed by this law that everyone was called to love and know the source of life. God in his sheer kindness drew close to her to bring her back to his fold. This experience was the foundation on which she built her life, and henceforth her existence was purposeful in Christ (2 Cor 12:2; Gal 2:20; Phil 1:21).[10] In the narrative, Hannah portrays Jesus as the Shepherd, a simile which one encounters in many verses of the Bible where God is described as the shepherd of his own people, and when Jesus depicts himself as the "good shepherd" (Ps 23:1; Ps 28:9; Isa 40:11; Matt 25:32; John 10:11). He is the shepherd who guides her to triumph over sin and to follow him into his kingdom. As a result, Hannah began to believe in Jesus because he revealed himself through the Holy Spirit and enlightened her on the meaning of life. Her desire for ultimate meaning was engraved on her heart; she was created in the image of God (Gen 1:27).[11]

> The root reason for human dignity lies in man's call to communion with God. From the very circumstance of his origin man is already invited to converse with God. For man would not exist were he not created by Gods love and constantly preserved by it; and he cannot live fully according to truth unless he freely acknowledges that love and devotes himself to His Creator.[12]

Hannah's quest to know God goes backs ages ago when our ancestors worshiped the mysterious through their various customs and cultures.[13] In Hannah's case she made this quest through the Bible. In the narrative she mentions biblical figures, like Abraham and Joseph, who journeyed with God.[14] At the same time, she highlights how God reveals himself to certain people, however through Jesus everybody is called to follow him. In Hannah's view God's revelation throughout history meant two

10. "To encounter the Lord is first of all to be encountered by the Lord. 'You did not choose me, but I chose you and appointed you that you should go and bear fruit' (John 15:16). This encounter we discover where the Lord lives, and what the mission is that has been entrusted to us" (Gutierrez, *We Drink from Our Own Wells,* 38).

11. *Catechism of the Catholic Church* 26–27.

12. Vatican Council II, *Gaudium et Spes* 19.

13. See Eliade, *Patterns in Comparative Religion; Catechism of the Catholic Church* 28; von Hugel in Downey, *Understanding Christian Spirituality,* 23–26.

14. See Hurnard, *Hinds' Feet,* 86.

points: in the first place the journey with God entailed that she possess an "upright heart," or as she calls it, the hearing heart.[15] This upright heart meant that she had to discern the signs of the Spirit in her experience and to be resolute in faith (Job 33:3; Ps 7:10; Prov 15:7). Secondly, God's revelation throughout history meant that Hannah valued the pedagogy of God. Throughout history he taught vital lessons to people, and now he would do the same to her.

> This, therefore, was the [object of the] long-suffering of God, that man, passing through all things, and acquiring the knowledge of moral discipline, then attaining to the resurrection from the dead, and learning by experience what is the source of his deliverance, may always live in a state of gratitude to the Lord, having obtained from Him the gift of incorruptibility, that he might love Him the more.[16]

Hannah's experience can be related to Rudolph Otto's (1869–1937) theological expression of the *mysterium tremendum*, a tender tide which is a tranquil mood of innermost worship.[17] This *mysterium tremendum* is the non-relational feature of our religious experiences. It is a moment of rapture when a person experiences God's mysterious holiness, which imparts feelings of wonder and reverence. Although Hannah tried on many occasions to convince herself to believe in Jesus by reading the Bible, it is only when the Bible penetrated her affections that she experienced the *numen* (sacred). The *numinous* created another feeling in Hannah called the creature-feeling toward God. Otto describes this creature-feeling as "the emotion of a creature, abased and overwhelmed by its own nothingness in contrast to that which is supreme above all creatures."[18] One thus concludes that when Hannah experienced these feelings she was drawn more closely to the mystery of Christ because "the desire to know does but increase this thirst,"[19] and then observed Jesus's command and call "follow me" (Matt 4:19; 9:9; John 1:43). Hannah wants to be in the presence of perfect goodness, gentleness, and intimacy mixed with majesty

---

15. See Hurnard, *Hearing Heart*; *Catechism of the Catholic Church* 30.

16. Irenaeus, *Against Heresies* 3.20.2.

17. Otto, *Idea of the Holy*, 12–13.

18. Ibid., 10.

19. De Caussade, *Abandonment to Divine Providence*, 9.

and wrath. Later on she rationalized this sentiment and formed her moral reasoning.[20]

Hannah depicts Much-Afraid with two physical defects, crippled feet and crooked mouth. These handicaps represent her lack of skill to solve problems (crippled feet) and her doubts (twisted mouth). What Hannah means is that even after her enlightenment she remained a sinner. As she was at the service of the Shepherd, her comportment left much to be desired. Probably the readers would represent these defects as symbols of the difficulties they have to face in their life. The transformation that Hannah alludes to concerns these two physical defects. Much-Afraid's desire to have hinds' feet was an expression to gain the necessary knowledge and skills to solve the problems, suppress her temptations, and follow the path of love and kindness. As a result, she envisages that she would remain endowed with God's grace and love. Hence, Hannah encourages the readers to accompany Much-Afraid in her journey to be able to be transformed into the image of Christ. This echoes to what Evagrius Ponticus articulates as the *passionlessness:*

> We shall recognise the signs of passionlessness through our thoughts (*logismoi*) during the day and through our dreams at night. And passionlessness is what we shall call the soul's health, and the soul's food is knowledge, which is the only means by which we shall ordinarily be united with the holy powers, seeing that the natural basis for our union with incorporeal beings is the similarity of our disposition to theirs.[21]
>
> The proof of *apatheia* is that the *nous* begins to behold its [own] proper gentle radiance; that it remains tranquil in the presence of visions during sleep; and that it looks at matters calmly.[22]

---

20. There is a scene in the allegorical narrative when Much-Afraid was constrained to ignore the *Shepherd's* call, yet the *seed of love* forced her to go beyond her fears and to search for Him in the depth of night. This can be related to what Saint John of the Cross writes, "On a dark night, Kindled in love with yearnings—oh, happy chance!—I went forth without being observed, My house being now at rest. In darkness and secure, By the secret ladder, disguised—oh, happy chance!—In darkness and in concealment, My house being now at rest. In the happy night, In secret, when none saw me, Nor I beheld aught, Without light or guide, save that which burned in my heart. This light guided me More surely than the light of noonday To the place where he (well I knew who!) was awaiting me—A place where none appeared" (John of the Cross, *Dark Night*, 1–4; Hurnard, *Hinds' Feet*, 48–54).

21. Evagrius, *Praktikos* 56.

22. Ibid., 64.

What the above author wishes to convey is the attitude when the subconscious and conscious are in harmony. When readers imagine Much-Afraid journeying from one place to another, they have to comprehend that these places are symbols, shadowing lessons from Hannah's life. One of these lessons deals with humbleness in life, a quality which Hannah blends with gratitude. According to her, individuals should not seek approval from others but approval from Jesus himself, who alone truly knows the hearts of man. This lesson of humility helped Hannah later in her journey, a journey full of contradictions.

Although this journey at first seemed smooth, in fact Hannah states that God revealed his power in the contradictions that followed, which were difficult to accept. When God intervened in her life she began to apprehend a fundamental truth about faith in Jesus: "the invisible and the apparent do not coincide with each other."[23] Much-Afraid's apparent difficulties which she encountered in the journey were perceived as a contradiction because she couldn't see through the intentions of the Shepherd. Faced with this situation her only option was to discern the events.[24] However, Hannah later stresses the point that if one embarks on a journey of transformation one needs to gradually trust in God. The readers are invited to search their heart and discern what God desires from them. They are urged to live out their life in God's plan even if their thoughts and emotions act against His will. For Hannah, it is only by doing God's will that one ultimately finds true meaning in life, even if trust involves daring into moments of obscurity and ambiguities. In the allegorical narrative we do note how Much-Afraid is gripped with anxiety regarding the strange places she had to travel to. One notes that Hannah is sensible to the daily experiences of Christians because she comprehends how human nature is fragile when faced with hardships. But she makes it clear that if one truly loves Jesus one must trust him and obey his command. Through obedience grace is poured forth. It is only through her obedience that Hannah experienced God and translated the contradictions into moments of love and grace. In spiritual theology this obedience is called perfection, where "it consists in doing the will of God, not in understanding His design."[25] Hannah gave credit to what is writ-

23. Costanza, "Abramo e l'esperienza della fede," 19; de Caussade, *Abandonment to Divine Providence*, 19.

24. See Hurnard, *Winged Life*, 14.

25. De Caussade depicts Mary the mother of Jesus as the perfect example of

ten in the letter to the Hebrews, namely, that "now faith is the assurance of the things hope for, the conviction of things not seen" (Heb 11:1).[26] Hannah accepted as true, that this journey she was to embark was a trial by God. However this test is not effective because God likes to inquire his followers, but because when the love of God is transcended it becomes a contrast to the old lifestyle. Indeed, by journeying with Jesus it becomes a test in itself.[27]

In Hannah's view, to be humble meant to be prudent and patient, a lesson she learned when Much-Afraid was at the Shores of Loneliness. Hannah exhorts that when one starts enjoying the fruits of the gradual transformation, one might become impatient and act precipitately in one's journey. It is true that God's grace strengthens the followers with a new understanding of the dynamics of sins, but Hannah advises to remain humble and not rush looking for glory in our achievements.[28] What Hannah is stating is that what really matters is our faith to gradually let God do the work.[29] This is not sheer passivity on the part of Hannah but an act of gratitude and humility before God. In this, Hannah seems to echo Saint Clement's advice:

> Learn to submit yourselves, laying aside the arrogant and proud stubbornness of your tongue. For it is better for you to be found little in the flock of Christ and to have your name on God's roll,

abandoning oneself to the will of God, even though she wasn't aware of his intentions or designs (Luke 1:25). He stresses on the word "over-shadowing" to highlight that Mary found God in the shadow that came on her (*Abandonment to Divine Providence*, 8).

26. See *Catechism of the Catholic Church* 150.

27. See Costanza, "Abramo e l'esperienza della fede," 21.

28. "I do not know whether I have put this clearly; self-knowledge is of such consequence that I would not have you careless of it, though you may be lifted to heaven in prayer, because while on earth nothing is more needful than humility. Therefore, I repeat, not only a *good* way, but the *best* of all ways, is to endeavor to enter first by the room where humility is practiced, which is far better than at once rushing on to the others. This is the right road;—if we know how easy and safe it is to walk by it, why ask for wings with which to fly? Let us rather try to learn how to advance quickly. I believe we shall never learn to know ourselves except by endeavoring to know God, for, beholding His greatness we are struck by our own baseness, His purity shows our foulness, and by meditating on His humility we find how very far we are from being humble" (Teresa of Avila, *Interior Castle*, 24).

29. Saint Macarius of Egypt stresses the role of our endeavors; he is explicit that the whole process of our development is the work of grace. "As a bee makes a honeycomb secretly in a sieve, so grace makes love of itself secretly in men's heart, changing them from bitterness to sweetness, from roughness to smoothness" (Tugwell, *Way of Perfection*, 50).

than to be in exceeding honor and yet be cast out from the hope of Him.[30]

And ye were all lowly in mind and free from arrogance, yielding rather than claiming submission, more glad to give than to receive, and content with the provisions which God supplieth. And giving heed unto His words, ye laid them up diligently in your hearts, and His sufferings were before your eyes.[31]

They all therefore were glorified and magnified, not through themselves or their own works or the righteous doing which they wrought, but through His will.[32]

Resolute, but at the same time humble and patient, Hannah also comments about the stress she endured by the Fearings. To make matters worse feelings of gloom, pride, bitterness and self-pity impacted on her. What is important is that we keep gradually transform ourselves by suppressing our temptations. This is a continuous struggle in our life.[33] In one of his homilies Saint Macarius of Egypt (c. 300–391) remarked that Christians are inclined to sin even after they have been immersed in the Holy Spirit:

When he first tasted grace, his soul revived and enjoyed a heavenly repose foreign to this world, so that he would know by experience the sweetness of goodness. But then, if his mind gets a little distracted or something, he is again filled with sin, so that he will be oppressed and learn by experience the bitterness of sin, and then he will seek refuge all the more speedily, seeking that ineffable consolation and repose. Then he obtains it again and revives and rests a little, but then, if he is careless, evil gains access and bitterly oppresses him, as grace gives it leave so that he may know by experience the sweetness and restfulness and consolation of grace and the bitterness and pain and oppressiveness of sin, so that, (if he wishes to be saved) he will the more earnestly flee the one and cleave wholly to grace.[34]

In the allegorical narrative Much-Afraid is assailed continuously by negative feelings. Hannah is aware that at times we fail to act and conduct

---

30. *First Epistle of Clement* 57.2.

31. *First Epistle of Clement* 8.

32. *First Epistle of Clement* 25–26.

33. This can be related with the Carmelite concept of being clothes in God's armor as a form of ascesism aiming for a purity of heart (Camilleri, *Carmel*, 30).

34. Tugwell, *Way of Perfection*, 49.

ourselves appropriately as Christ desires. Although Much-Afraid proceeded with her journey, meaning that at this journey she did not commit any sins, Hannah still teaches us that during our journey we are often tempted to ignore the Shepherd's teachings. One notes that Hannah is conveying her view that God does not intervene when we are being tempted to sin. However, through these temptations she matures in her love toward God. This is part of God's purification plan for her benefit. Hannah not only views this plan as grace showered on her in order to enlighten her but also as a way that enables the flourishing of Grace in her heart until it becomes a "flower of love."[35] This "flower" teaches the Christian to change the negative thoughts and to be conformed to God's charity. One notes that when Much-Afraid is portrayed descending into Egypt and observed the three tasks at the pyramid she was in fact accentuating the process of transformation. On observing these tasks the reader has to understand that when God bestows grace on us, things are not made easier immediately. On the contrary, the immediate result is an increase in tension. Each of the tasks at the pyramid are stages of a whole process. By the "crushing of grain" (Isa 28:27) Hannah meant that God would be examining her inner feelings and thoughts and would be purging her from her immoral desires and passions. Following this he would "mould her like clay" (Jer 18) into his image. Finally he would bestow on her "precious jewels" (Isa 54:12), denoting his grace and love. Hannah believes that if she participates in this process she would gain knowledge about the "victorious living" (Rev 2:7). She correlates with what Saint Macarius of Egypt states in the following abstract:

> We have to force ourselves to the utmost of our ability to practice the virtues, but our own efforts will not bring us success. We cannot deliver ourselves from the tension between the two "spirits" at work in us; what we can and must do is refrain from cultivating both these spirits. We must resolutely identify ourselves only with the good, and we must go on doing this however much out thoughts and even our actions are still controlled by sin. If we persevere in this inner struggle, then the Lord will himself "avenge us against our enemies" and give us the "great healing."[36]

---

35. Hurnard, *Hinds' Feet*, 114.

36. Tugwell, *Way of Perfection*, 51; see also Augustine, *On Grace and Free Will* 5.6, 10.

In Hannah's narrative one finds a description of another experience she came across in her spiritual life. When Much-Afraid was immersed in the Mist she lost her way and didn't see clearly the tracks of her journey. One may say that this corresponds to what Saint John of the Cross describes as the "Dark Night." Here both the "sensual" and the "spiritual" nature of the human person (soul) are purified through the action of God's love. In this particular state, the soul knows she is no more in control; she is actively passive, abandoned to God's grace. Thus she cannot keep track of her journey. In this very particular and painful spiritual state, the abandoned soul does experiences aridity and a sense of being somewhat lost.

> This night, which, as we say, is contemplation, produces in spiritual persons two kinds of darkness or purgation, corresponding to the two parts of man's nature—namely, the sensual and the spiritual. And thus the one night or purgation will be sensual, wherein the soul is purged according to sense, which is subdued to the spirit; and the other is a night or purgation which is spiritual, wherein the soul is purged and stripped according to the spirit, and subdued and made ready for the union of love with God.[37]

According to Saint John only in the absence of consolations—material and spiritual—is the soul purified, and only then does it experience the bright light of God's grace as darkness. It is as if the pure divine light blinds the enamoured soul. In such a state our senses are rendered weak and our spirits strengthened and transformed to fully enjoy the gifts of God.[38] One can compare this state to what the children of Israel experienced in the wilderness when being fed on food, which tasted insipid to their palate. Yet it was this food which invigorated them and strengthened them in their journey. In this spiritual state contemplative souls behold God in poverty and dark contemplation. The soul feeds on the new food which the inner spirit provides, and matures to find God even in the absence of what satisfies the soul's appetites.[39] Like Saint Anthony the Abbot in the desert and later on Saint Catherine of Siena, Hannah cried out,

---

37. John of the Cross, *Dark Night* 8.1; Bernard, *Il Dio dei mistici*, 389.

38. John of the Cross, *Dark Night* 8.4; "the more hidden the divine operations beneath an outwardly repulsive appearance, the more visible it is to the eyes of faith" (de Caussade, *Abandonment*, 21).

39. John of the Cross, *Dark Night* 8.6.

"Where were you, Lord, when my heart was crying out for you?"[40] In this situation Hannah encourages us to continue journeying with the little we see, and keep waiting for when God would appear again.[41] At a certain stage, Hannah realized that God was in her heart, and in such a state she received the same answer Saint Catherine did when God answered her and said, "I was in your heart."[42]

These spiritual or mystical states made Hannah realise that true transformation requires time, suffering, and sorrow, and that the hardships suffered would eventually bear fruits (Luke 6:44).[43] In fact, the companions of Much-Afraid were Suffering and Sorrow. One notes here the connection between Hannah's theology and Pauline theology. When Saint Paul speaks about suffering he is convinced that sorrow wouldn't separate him from God (Rom 8:38–39). Hannah refers to Paul's experience and stresses that suffering is an essential element in our journey in this world. She is convinced that in suffering God is present. Through her weakness and sorrow she was rendered splendid and given the name Grace and Glory. She began to believe in Paul's words: "Therefore I am content with weaknesses, insults, hardships, persecutions, and calamities for the sake of Christ; for whenever I am weak, then I am strong" (2 Cor 12:10). It is perhaps interesting to note that in applying Paul's words to her life more intimately, in her autobiographies she highlights this quote: "My grace is sufficient for you, for power is made perfect in weakness" (2 Cor 12:8).[44] For Hannah this quote particularly meant a divine invitation to participate in Christ's passion. She envisages that she has to be

---

40. Capua, *La vita di St. Caterina di Siena,* 67–68; "Where wert thou? Why didst thou not appear at the beginning to make my pains to cease?' And a voice came to him, 'Antony, I was here, but I waited to see thy fight; wherefore since thou hast endured, and hast not been worsted, I will ever be a succour to thee, and will make thy name known everywhere" (Anthanasius, *Life of St. Antony* 10).

41. In the allegory there is a scene when Much-Afraid utters, "'O my Lord! . . . I thank thee for leading me here. Behold me, here I am, empty . . . but waiting thy time to be filled to the brim with the flood-tide of Love" (Hurnard, *Hinds' Feet,* 97); this relates to the "empty hands" of Saint Therese of Lisieux in De Meester, *With Empty Hands,* 57.

42. "Io ero nel tuo cuore" (Capua, *La vita di St. Caterina di Siena,* 67–68).

43. "Maria e un'immagine del cammino mistico, al quale Dio ci ha chiamati. I Padri della Chiesa dicono che noi stessi diventiamo madre di Cristo e che nel nostro cuore avviene la nascita di Dio. La nascita di Dio ci trasforma, sensa annullare le nostre debolezze umane. Restiamo il roveto, l'uomo debole, per parte nostra vuoti e disseccati. E, nonstant cio, appare in noi la gloria di Dio" (Grun, *Il coraggio di trasformarsi,* 10).

44. See Hurnard, *Hearing Heart,* 19.

willing to experience what Jesus himself endured. Through her suffering her carnal nature is put to death in the hope of being transformed
into a new person, reflecting the resurrection of Jesus (Phil 3:10–11).[45]
Inspired by the theology of Saint Paul, Hannah believes that individuals
given to the spiritual life suffer together with Him to be glorified with
Him. "I consider that the sufferings of this present time are not worth
comparing with the glory about to be revealed to us" (Rom 8:17–18). She
believed what Paul said about Jesus, that He who was loved by God was
resurrected from death. This firm belief applies to all those who believe in
Jesus, because they have been adopted in His family (2 Cor 4:14). Before
entering the High Places, Much-Afraid had to make the highest sacrifice:
to offer her Longing-to-be-Loved. This longing was perceived by Hannah
as contradicting her yearning to be with Christ. Upon entering spiritual
darkness Hannah couldn't understand God's will. At first, she tried to find
excuses, but later she obeyed in silence. She realized that God really loved
her and understood the power of faith to save our soul. One notes that the
notion of sacrifice in the allegory denotes that obedience is not only an
ethical behaviour which Hannah looked up to, but it is a conviction that
God demanded everything she possessed, and that He would provide the
best provisions to the soul (1 Cor 10:13).[46] In doing so, God manifested
his grace that he gives life to a dead soul.[47] In fact, when Much-Afraid's
impure love was eliminated the "flower of love" blossomed in her heart,
and she was transformed into Grace and Glory (1 Cor 10:31). The "flower
of love" can be correlated to the Holy Spirit who guides us. Hannah believes that when the Holy Spirit is allowed to guide our heart and spirit
individuals become a new creation. This new creation in Christ makes

45. See Hurnard, *Winged Life*, 30–31; Hurnard, *Mountain of Spices*, 71. When Much-Afraid's last sacrifice occurred, she fell in a long sleep. After three days she woke up and was transformed into *Grace and Glory*. This explicitly reminds us about the three days Jesus was buried before he resurrected (Hurnard, *Hinds' Feet*, 223).

46. "The first great duty of souls called by God to this state is the absolute and entire surrender of themselves to Him" (De Caussade, *Abandonment to Divine Providence*, 61).

47. "Vivo sin vivir en mi [I live yet do not live in me]" (John of the Cross, *Poems*, 62). "A Sacrifice, according to some theologians, has two elements, *oblation* (or offering) and *immolation* (or destruction) of the victim. This latter element, they say, is necessary for a true sacrifice because it demonstrates more completely God's supreme dominion over creation and man's absolute submission to Him. Such a sacrifice symbolizes complete self-surrender on the part of man; it is an act of adoration proper to God alone (techni-cally called *latria*)" (Moore, *Christ, the Church, and the Soul*, 69).

us remain in him, and the perfect *koinonia*, that is, the communion or intimate relationship we have with God and Jesus Christ is formed.[48] This echoes Paul's words in the second letter to the Corinthians:

> So if anyone is in Christ, there is a new creation: everything old has passed away; see, everything has become new! All this is from God, who reconciled us to himself through Christ, and has given us the ministry of reconciliation (2 Cor 5:17–18).

This new transformation meant that Hannah's natural love was substituted with unselfish love—charity. Hitherto her love is focused only on God, and her only desire is to offer all her possessions and achievements to the "Beloved." While neglecting her own interests, her only desire is to please and obey Him. Also, Saint John of the Cross in the *Spiritual Canticle* made the same observation when he said that "it is a property of perfect love to be unwilling to take anything for self, nor does it attribute anything to self, but all to the Beloved. If we find this characteristic in base loves, how much more in love of God, where reason so strongly obliges us to this."[49]

HANNAH'S FRACTURED SPIRITUALITY

From the narrative readers can derive several spiritual and moral benefits. Besides presenting Christ as the central aspiration of the individual's life, it imparts subtle extreme moral teachings of which one should be aware.[50]

What might concern readers in Much-Afraid's journey is the author's approach to "negative" feelings and thoughts in relation to Jesus which are mentioned in the narrative, primarily, pessimism, gloom, fear, spiteful, pride, self-pity, bitterness, and resentment, and which are symbolized as the Fearings. It appears that Hannah believes that these feelings are contrary to the "positive" feelings offered to us through Christ's mercy. One concludes that Hannah examines feelings and thoughts from

---

48. See Hurnard, *Winged Life*, 33.

49. John of the Cross, *Spiritual Canticle*, A stanza 23.1; B stanza 32.2, in *Collected Works*, 535.

50. "Immaturity, irresponsibility, brute exercise of power, and irrational behavior should signal caution, even and especially when appeal is made to a higher order or spiritual principle in an effort to justify them" (Downey, *Understanding Christian Spirituality*, 8; Gula, *Call to Holiness*, 2).

a dualistic and conflicting standpoint.[51] These incidents in the narrative bear out this attitude.

Firstly, one notes that the reason why Much-Afraid decided to leave her dwelling at the Valley of Humiliation was the torment and misery which prevailed at that place. To regain happiness her only way out was to escape, and likewise the Shepherd gave her moral support.[52] The second incidence occurred during Much-Afraid's journey to the High Places. On her route the Fearings did their utmost to disrupt her journey. Faced with this situation Much-Afraid tried to ignore and suppress her fears by singing stanzas of songs and by stopping her ears.[53] Most astounding is the last scene when Much-Afraid surrenders her "natural-human love" to God, and the Shepherd disguised as a Priest penetrates her heart and gashes out this love with its deep roots and reduces it to ashes.[54]

These three events emphasize a crescendo as to the manner the author responds to these feelings. Hannah relates "negative" feelings to the disposition of the world and to humanity. In the end, the transformation which Hannah recommends is related to the elimination of anything which is of a sinful human nature.[55] She perceives the world, in general, as corrupt, and whatever it offers goes against God's will. Thus, she believes that if one desires to be truly free and nearer to Christ, one must renounce as much as possible anything the world offers and what one possesses. Hannah believes that due to our human nature one should suppress one's

51. See Hurnard, *Mountain of Spices*, 85–87; Hurnard, *Walking among the Unseen*, 13–18; "Major philosophical traditions of Western culture have tended to explain the human body by distinguishing it from, and often opposing it to, the soul (or spirit or mind). The boundary between body and soul, in such views, constitutes a fissure within the human individual, and it prevents full union between persons. . . . In this binary division, the soul is frequently the truly 'human,' while the body constitutes an unfortunate and temporary limitation on the human spirit (signified by famous metaphors like container and contained, prison and imprisoned)" (Farley, *Framework*, 112).

52. See Hurnard, *Hinds' Feet on High Places*, 21; *Mountain of Spices*, 13.

53. See Hurnard, *Hinds' Feet on High Places* 147, 160.

54. Ibid., 208; Hurnard, *Mountain of Spices*, 60.

55. As a Quaker Hannah related with what George Fox speaks in his Quaker journal: "Be still and cool in thy own mind and spirit from thy own thoughts, and then thou wilt feel the principle of God to turn thy mind to the Lord God, whereby thou wilt receive his strength and power from whence life comes, to allay all tempest, against blusterings and storms. That is it which moulds up into patience, into innocency, into soberness, into stillness, into stayedness, into quietness, up to God, with his power" (Durham, *Spirit of the Quakers*, 38).

own passions. Moreover, these "negative" feelings are rooted in our sinful human nature and infringe on our growth toward fulfilling God's charity in us.

This was finally expressed at the altar scene. Hannah shows her true understanding of God's love by acting in a way different through her rejection of the impure carnal love. In her view carnal-human love is self-seeking, controlled by passions, while God's love is established on his grace and is self-giving. Thus, if one gives way to these negative thoughts and feelings one would sin in thoughts and actions.[56] In the allegory she develops these convictions figuratively, however in her later journal, *Kingdom of Love*, she amplifies her arguments:

> I was to be transformed by a renewed mind. This was the glorious salvation He promised me, complete liberty and release from the tyranny of self reigning in my thought life.[57]
>
> If one never allows irritated, annoying critical or unloving thoughts to remain in the mind a moment, however strongly they may clamour for permission to remain, and if only creative love thinking is the habit of our thought life, nobody will be able to see through us or in us, thoughts are not there and our whole outward manner will be transformed.[58]
>
> Again and again self proved overwhelmingly stronger than my will, able to smash through every barrier I had tried to set up of self-control, reckoning the old life to be a corpse, yes, and even calling upon the Lord to deliver me.[59]
>
> As our Lord takes over control of more and more of the realm of the mind, so the dark and cloudy periods should become more and more rare, for darkness belongs to sin. . . . As with the creation of the earth, so with the new creation in our spirits, the evening and the morning make up the day. First there is the darkness and chaos of Self-dominion, and then the dawning into the full light and sunshine of perfect day. Outwardly our circumstance may be

---

56. See Hurnard, *Mountain of Spices*, 45, 46; Hurnard, *Walking among the Unseen*, 21. St. Justin looks at the altar quiet differently from Hannah, "The only honor that is worth of him is not to consume by fire what he has brought into being for our sustenance, but to use it for ourselves and those who need, and with gratitude to him to offer thanks by praises and hymns for our creation" (Quasten, *Patrology*, 1:218).

57. Hurnard, *Kingdom of Love*, 38.

58. Ibid., 53.

59. Ibid., 57.

gloomy and dark indeed, but more and more the inner reaction to these difficulties and trails will be one of joy and peace.[60]

Many factors could have contributed to her understanding of faith. The family's Puritan lifestyle, which originally was repulsive to Hannah, could have played a part. In fact, she adopted this lifestyle after she had experienced Jesus and started to act more in line with what others taught her.[61] Moreover, her earlier experience of misery also had an impact on her. One notes that Hannah experienced two different sets of feelings from an extreme point of view, from continuous depressing feelings to those positive feelings when she experienced God's love. Hannah concluded that God only bestows positive feelings. This overshadowed her missionary service which she carried out with fervour and passion at Palestine. One should also be aware that she was taught that those who did not believe in Jesus would not be saved and, if they died, would end up in hell.[62] However, in spite of her religious education, Hannah still felt unhappy, and in this state she thought she was sinful; negative thoughts kept creeping into her mind about the essential theology lesson that grace alone was sufficient.[63] It is to be pointed out that this change in attitude could have contributed to her unorthodox theology, more so when she had to face other dilemmas. After she published *Hinds' Feet on High Places*, Hannah revealed to the public her concept that everyone would be saved, even sinners. To her way of thinking, God in his absolute goodness and mercy wouldn't allow anyone to be lost.[64] Her ideas were vehemently disputed by her Christian friends, and she was judged as holding the heterodox belief in universalism.[65]

60. Ibid., 77; Hurnard, *Winged Life*, 69, 71; Hurnard, *Walking among the Unseen*, 52; Hurnard, *Inner Man*, 54–60.

61. See Hurnard, *Hearing Heart*, 9; Wood, *Hannah Hurnard*, 32.

62. See Hurnard, *Kingdom of Love*, 11, 32; even from an allegorical point of view Hannah can be seen as somewhat patronizing those who were from a different religion: Hurnard, *Mountain of Spices*, 83–85; Hurnard, *Walking among the Unseen*, 39–40. This somehow created a tension in Hannah's life. On one hand her Quaker upbringing is founded a lot on the idea of equality, yet the evangelical influence made a difference between those who believed in Jesus and those who did not.

63. See Hurnard, *Kingdom of Love*, 30, 33, 34.

64. See Hurnard, *Thou Shalt Remember*. 92–94.

65. Fisher, *From High Places to Heresy*; Anders, *Story of Hannah Hurnard*, 163–166; Hurnard, *Winged Life*, 23, 26.

However, one has to understand Hannah's past before one can judge her so casually.[66] Without delving into the merit of her drastic theological drift, what is crucial for this study to note is that Hannah began to consider God as a merciful father who loves each person regardless of their religion. Hannah began to understand that she was pardoned by God and accordingly started questioning her image of God. She no longer believed in Him as a stern judge but as a merciful father.[67] Despite her unorthodox doctrine, one should also be open to her reasons rather than judge and condemn her. Most probably her extreme attitude toward the world and human feelings could have made her subscribe to paranormal superstitious beliefs or what is known today as New Age philosophy.[68] One notes that Hannah focused only on her own feelings and needs, and at one point decided to become a vegetarian and later a fruitarian.[69] Regrettably she veered into an illusionary world detached from the realities of existence. What she needed in her dilemmas was spiritual guidance, but unfortunately she never met someone who could enlighten her.[70]

One can recall here the admonitions of the Desert Fathers against embarking onto the spiritual journey alone. They were appalled by imaginary and fanciful spirituality uncorrelated to human experience: "If you see a young man going up to heaven by his own will, grab his leg and pull him down again."[71]

Hannah's effort directed toward life in union with Christ is mostly admired. Nevertheless, maturity cannot occur with a drastic orientation where one separates affections, thoughts, and the entire creation from the saving grace of God. It is to be pointed out that the human being is endowed with the power of free-will.[72] However, when one adopts an

---

66. Anders, *Story of Hannah Hurnard*, 178–183.

67. Hurnard, *Kingdom of Love*, 86.

68. Hurnard, *Inner Man*; Hurnard, *Steps to the Kingdom*; Hurnard, *Walking among the Unseen*, 50–51.

69. Wood, *Hannah Hurnard*, 150–159.

70. "There was no mediating agency between worshiper and God in Quaker meeting. There was no one in the Society of Friends to tell you what you had to do, nor was there a right or wrong way to practice faith there" (*Quaker Spirituality*, vii).

71. Hurnard, *Way of Imperfection*, 16

72. See Radcliffe, *What Is the Point?* 29–48; Gula, *Call to Holiness*, 13–14; Aschenbrenner, *Quickening the Fire*, 3.

extreme perception regarding life, one has to bear the resulting consequences which affect the soul.

> With the phenomenological method . . . we can study experiences of morality, religion or simply what it is to be human, and draw from them a significant enrichment of our knowledge. Yet we must not forget that these analyses implicitly presuppose the reality of the Absolute Being and also the reality of being human, that is, being a creature. If we do not set out from such "realist" presuppositions, we end up in a vacuum.[73]

In reality, the Christian tradition is nourished on the concept that body, soul, and spirit, though distinct, are not separated but are so united as to give unity of nature. In fact, human beings yearn for an integrated lifestyle where neither the body nor the soul nor the spirit is undermined. In Karl Rahner's view,

> Human beings are *spirit* in the world. *Spirit* here "names" that dimension of the human person which is distinct from but not opposed to the material, i.e., the body. The person is properly understood as a unity, a whole, rather than as a hybrid of competing parts of body and soul, flesh and spirit, mind and matter.[74]

Believers no longer allow a disengaged faith from their life but tend to lead a lifestyle which is progressively in line with that of the kingdom of God. At the same time, they should not give up their daily activities, nor neglect their physical and spiritual needs.[75] Before judging, one needs to ponder what Origen declares about the "bride" in Song of Solomon: "to know thy self."[76] Only through self-awareness individuals can start debating on the sanctification of the entire human race.[77] Correspond-

73. John Paul II, *Memory and Identity*, 13.

74. Rahner in Downey, *Understanding Christian Spirituality*, 33.

75. "In the light of Christ, when natural beauty of creation is in harmony with the will of the Creator, it leads to the contemplation of heavenly order" (John of the Cross, *Ascent of Mt. Carmel*, 37–38).

76. *Song of Songs*, 128–139; "Il primo ambito nel quale si manifesta la potenza dello Spirito e quello della conoscenza interiore. Secondo un'osservazzione antecedente, lo Spirito infatti puo essere considerato l'interiorita di ogni cosa: di Dio, del mondo e dell'io (1 Cor 2:10–16)" (Bernard, *Il Dio dei mistici*, 40). "Nel suo studio su san Bernardo, Etienne Gilson mostra che il riconoscimento da parte dell'uomo della propia dignita oscurata dal peccato appartiene a cio che si puo chiamare 'il socratismo cristiano,' fondato sul vecchio adagio 'Conosci te stesso'" (Bernard, *Il Dio dei mistici*, 39).

77. "How I wish that I could make them understand that just as the good and the

ingly, this conviction can be deduced from the Bible. In revealing himself to Abraham, God promises:

> I will make of you a great nation, and I will bless you, and make your name great, so that you will be a blessing. I will bless those who bless you, and the one who curses you I will curse; and in you all the families of the earth shall be blessed. (Gen 12:2–3)

Following this blessing, Abraham's circumstances and the people around him flourished in many aspects. This included physical and psychological well-being, the development of a stable community, and the enjoyment of the creation's gifts. Through Abraham, God revealed himself and moulded historical events. Therefore, being blessed by God denotes leading a decent life and respecting and loving others. It means cultivating a presence of God in the here and now.[78] This attitude would not render a person individualist, but would cultivate a spirituality toward God and others.[79]

The desire of Christians to be happy in their inmost feelings and surroundings should be grounded on the doctrine of the Incarnation, the mystery when God became fully human without sin. Jesus, the Son of God and equally God like the Father, was made flesh, and through Him God continues to relate with humans. The "Word became flesh and lived among us" (John 1:14).[80] Karl Rahner states that the Incarnation is the historical episode which conveys divine connotations, because in this mystery God assumed a human nature and accordingly sanctified all

---

bad thief has the same things to do and to suffer; so also two person, one of whom is worldly and the other leading an interior and wholly spiritual life have, neither of them, anything different to do or to suffer; but that one is sanctified and attains eternal happiness by submission to Your holy will in those very things by which the other is damned because he does them to please himself, or endures them with reluctance and rebellion" (De Caussade, *Abandonment to Divine Providence*, 17). "Thomas Merton comes to mind as one who lived as a contemplative but with an intense spirituality for the deepest yearning for life. . . . It [contemplative spirituality] risks reducing spirituality to a myopic 'me and God' exercises of one's soul without including the lives of those who suffer" (Gula, *Call to Holiness*, 14).

78. Downey, *Understanding Christian Spirituality*, 30.

79. *Guadium et spes* 57, 59, 63, 64; "Il primo luogo va notato che, conformemente alla tradizione scritturistica, la spiritualita giudeo-cristiana ha sempre stabilito una continuita tra il Dio creatore che lo spettacolo della nature e la legge morale disvelano alla conoscenza dell'uomo, e il Dio dell'alleanza che si china verso l'uomo" (Bernard, *Il Dio dei mistici*, 75).

80. *Catechism of the Catholic Church* 461.

creation.[81] Being God, he took to himself a complete human nature like ours and made it his own. He is therefore one God-Person with two natures, Divine and Human.[82] If one thinks that Jesus was part man or part God, then the separation between the material and the supernatural is accepted, but Jesus was truly God and man at the same time. This mystery denotes a complete unity between body, soul, and spirit.[83] Through the Paschal Mystery this fusion is revealed.

> The Paschal Mystery thus becomes the definitive measure of man's existence in the world created by God. In this mystery, not only is eschatology truth revealed to us. . . . There also shined forth a light to enlighten the whole human existence in its temporal dimension, and this light is then reflected onto the created world. Christ, through his Resurrection, has so to speak "justified" the work of creation, and especially the creation of man.[84]

The Trinity and the Incarnation are connected mysteries of faith. A central doctrine of Christian theology is the doctrine of the Trinity. This states that God is one substance but with three distinct co-equal and co-eternal persons: the Father, the Son, and the Holy Spirit. God the Father exists from all eternity without deriving His origin from either of the other persons. God the Son is born of the Father from all eternity but without being dependent on or inferior to the Father. God the Holy Spirit proceeds from the Father and the Son as from one Principle from all eternity without inferiority.[85] Since each person is God, each has all the

81. Kelly, *Karl Rahner*, 96–110; "Il fatto piu mirabile, del resto, in questa disposizione divina, e che l'elevazione alla vita nello Spirito si opera grazie all'attaccamento, che non si puo non chiamare 'carnale,' all'umanita del Verbo incarnato" (Bernard, *Il dio dei mistici*, 45).

82. "'Hypostatic Union': In the *One Person* of Jesus Christ there are *two natures*, the nature of God and the nature of man" (Moore, *Christ, the Church, and the Soul*, 39).

83. *Catechism of the Catholic Church* 464, 470, 472, 475; "We believe that God creates our bodies and drew near to us in Jesus Christ, flesh and blood like us. Our central sacrament is the sharing of his body. We believe that he was raised bodily from the grave and that we shall be too" (Radcliffe, *What Is the Point?* 87).

84. John Paul II, *Memory and Identity*, 27; "And he comes into our world, taking to himself the reality of our fresh, and dying and rising again in that flesh, so forging a unity between flesh and spirit" (Ignatius of Antioch in *Ways of Imperfection*, 3). "San Bernardo non si attarda a descrivere il processo di distacco dal senso per passare all'adesione della fede che si appoggia sull'unico Parola. Per lo meno ne ha percepito la necessita. In una formula molto concisa, dice all'anima: Abbi fede, e sei bella" (Bernard, *Il dio dei mistici*, 38).

85. See Moore, *Christ, the Church, and the Soul*, 26–27

divine attributes or perfections. All the dealings of God with creatures are performed through the Holy Trinity. The Son was the Word made flesh and descended in this world to unite us with the Father. After His passion, resurrection, and ascent to heaven, the Holy Spirit continues to enlighten and guide the human mind and sustains hearts with the Truth.[86]

Moreover, one cannot disregard the fact that human beings were made in the image and the likeliness of God. In both body and soul the human is endowed with the spirit of God. In its entirety a person can be called a creature in the image of God.[87] Hence, even the body has its due importance in the eyes of God.[88] In its entirety, the human person becomes a living temple of the Holy Spirit.[89] On this point, Saint Thomas Aquinas commented that grace did not inhibit or supercede nature but instead perfects it, opening the door to prospects of a more authentic life based on justice among creation.[90] Moreover, Gustavo Gutierrez (1928–)

86. *Catechism of the Catholic Church* 234, 253, 254; "by Sanctifying Grace we become 'sons of God and, if sons, heirs also: heirs indeed of God and joint-heirs with Christ' (Rom. 8:16). We become 'partakers of the Divine Nature' (2 Pet 1:4), so that the Blessed Trinity and especially the Holy Ghost may be said to inhabit the soul" (Moore, *Christ, the Church, and the Soul*, 29). "The Holy Spirit guides the Church through the world and through the course of history. Thanks to this gist of the Risen Christ, the Lord remains with us as events pass by; it is through the Spirit that we can recognize in Christ the meaning of human events. The Holy Spirit gives us the Church, communion and the community constantly convened, renewed, and sent forwards towards the accomplishment of the Kingdom of God" (Benedict XVI, "Current Crisis").

87. "Irenaeus makes a distinction between *imago Dei* and *similitude Dei*. Man is by nature, by his immaterial soul, an image of God. The *similitude Dei* is the similarity to God of a supernatural kind which Adam possessed by a voluntary act of God's goodness. This *similitude Dei* is effected by the divine Pneuma" (Quasten, *Patrology*, 1:311).

88. *Catechism of the Catholic Church* 357, 358, 362, 364; Gula, *Call to Holiness*, 65–106.

89. "The body is not seen as the enemy or a prison of the spirit, but celebrated as the Spirit's temple. Through Jesus' birth, life, death, and Resurrection, the human body has become part of life of God" (Kelly, "Through the Church Year," 6).

90. Gutierrez, *Theology of Liberation*, 35; Gustavo Gutierrez also writes about the Pauline spirituality between body and soul (*We Drink from Our Own Wells*, 56–71). "The fact that humans are embodied spirits, inspirited bodies, is the glory of our species and the basis of its vulnerability. We live incarnated in a world that is revelatory of the sacred. We are gifted in body and spirit by all creation's speaking to us God's word and providing for us a home where we may find sustenance and joy" (Farley, *Framework for Christian Sexual Ethics*, 117). "There are two major frameworks in which Christian theologians have tried to think about the human body: the framework of creation, fall, and redemption, and the framework of creation and consummation. If Augustine adopts the first of these, Thomas Aquinas adopts the second. . . . Bodily creation and consummation are located within a context of belief that all things come forth from God with the destiny

addresses God as part of our history and relates the human being as a secularization agent of our Creator.

> Biblical faith does indeed affirm the existence of creation as distinct from the Creator; it is the proper sphere of humankind, and God has proclaimed humankind lord of this creation. *Wordliness,* therefore, is a must, a necessary condition for an authentic relationship between humankind and nature, among human beings themselves, and finally, between human kind and God.[91]

A prominent Saint who sought to accentuate the presence of "God in all things, loving Him in all creatures and all creatures in Him" is Saint Ignatius of Loyola (1491–1556).[92] In his *Spiritual Exercises* he instructs the Christian how to incorporate faith with life.[93] This attempt, to find God in all periods of history and of creation, can be named *contemplation in actions.*[94] It develops in an inner freedom when the individual in each and every situation discovers God. This is the catalyst of a spirituality which might be described as the power for active apostles. Ignatius's spirituality is based and sustained on the discernment of spirits. During prayers and during spiritual guidance the individual becomes skilled at discerning the presence of God in the real experience.[95] In the *Spiritual*

---

to return to God. Aquinas's rendering of this belief is in metaphysical and cosmic terms. . . . For both, however the body is one with the soul in the human person, and the *body* as well as the soul is engaged by God's grace" (Farley, *Framework for Christian Sexual Ethics,* 131).

91. Gutierrez, *Theology of Liberation,* 42. "God, infinitely perfect and blessed in himself, in a plan of sheer goodness freely created man to make him share in his own blessed life. For this reason, at every time and in every place, God draws close to man. He calls man to seek him, to know him, to love him with all his strength. He calls together all men, scattered and divided by sin, into the unity of his family, the Church. To accomplish this, when the fullness of time had come, God sent his Son as Redeemer and Savior. In his Son and through him, he invites men to become, in the Holy Spirit, his adopted children and thus heirs of his blessed life" (*Catechism of the Catholic Church* 1.1).

92. Ignatius of Loyola, *Autobiography,* 99.

93. Ignatius of Loyola, *Spiritual Exercises.*

94. "There is not a moment in which God does not present Himself under the cover of some pain to be endured, of some consolation to be enjoyed, or of some duty to be performed. All that takes within us, around us, or through us, contains and conceals His divine action" (De Caussade, *Abandonment to Divine Providence,* 19; Aschenbrenner, *Quickening the Fire,* 7–15).

95. "The call of the Spirit of Christ is to be discerned wherever and whenever human beings are striving to promote authentic growth in knowledge, in freedom, and in loving relationship to others" (Downey, *Understanding Christian Spirituality,* 31, 40–44).

Exercises Ignatius counsels us that in one's journey toward holiness one should unite the body with soul. Rather than looking eerily on the body, one realises how fragile and limited our life is compared to God, but instead of dismissing it one should observe the command of God to share the goods of the world and to bear in mind that after this life there is the final destiny to each of us. The *Spiritual Exercises* teach us how to purify these affections.[96] This matter perplexed Hannah. However, this dilemma was not Hannah's sole preoccupation; others tried to find a way to deal with sin which rendered the world depraved. Ignatius provides the equilibrium: feelings are given their due importance but are not to be barred or permitted to dominate the individual. Even Saint John of the Cross in his *Ascent of Mount Carmel* seems to be highlighting this standing.[97] Feelings are to be purified when the senses and the spirit are experiencing the "dark night." In all these instances the lesson imparted is to seek the roots of our affections.

> Hence if anyone wants to know how this unhappy situation can be overcome, Christians will tell him that all human activity, constantly imperilled by man's pride and deranged self-love, must be purified and perfected by the power of Christ's cross and resurrection. For redeemed by Christ and made a new creature in the Holy Spirit, man is able to love the things themselves created by God, and ought to do so. He can receive them from God and respect and reverence them as flowing constantly from the hand of God. Grateful to his Benefactor for these creatures, using and enjoying them in detachment and liberty of spirit, man is led forward into a true possession of them, as having nothing, yet possessing all things. "All are yours, and you are Christ's, and Christ is God's" (1 Cor 3:22–23).[98]

Individuals are to be conscious of their feelings and should reflect on the roots of these feelings. One has to note that feelings are signals and not a cause.[99] Only when they are accepted and offered to God can one be healed and transformed. In this process the "good" feeling ameliorates (consolation) while the "negative" feeling undergoes an enlightened

96. See Aumann, *Spiritual Theology*, 177–207
97. John of the Cross, *Ascent of Mount Carmel.*
98. *Gaudium et spes,* 37.
99. *Catechism of the Catholic Church* 1767.

experience to mature (desolation).[100] One notes that discernment and spiritual guidance are essential in this process. Through discernment one ponders deeply on the consolations or desolations that the heart receives from God, while in spiritual guidance the person seeks counsel from someone mature in the patterns of God's activity.[101]

From this angle the notion of salvation differs from that of the un-believers. Salvation becomes a qualitative characteristic when it includes the human experiences, transforms it, and leads it to its fullness in Christ. The centrality of salvation remains on Christ who through his redemp-tion transmutes the universe and makes it possible for the individual to fulfil his existence. Hence, salvation comprises every characteristic of hu-manity, body and spirit.[102] Moreover, through salvation one is a witness of Christ rather than one who exhorts people to believe.

This is attained through the sacraments of the Catholic Church, mainly in the celebration of the Lord's Supper, the location of the genuine mission of the Church. The original intent of the Eucharist is to celebrate the gift of the salvific action of God in humanity.[103] This salvation which was brought about by Christ through his passion and resurrection brings us into fellowship with one another and with God, and reminds us that grace overcomes sin. The Eucharist, the sacrament commemorating the Last Supper in which bread and wine are consecrated and consumed, symbolize the gifts of creation.[104] One notes that it is from the gifts of creation that God communicates with us and encourages us to build a just world. Congar believed that through the Eucharist the *koinonia* expresses its true and highest meaning.

> First it signified the common ownership of the goods necessary
> for earthly existence: "Never forget to show kindness and to share

100. "If I am free, I can make good or bad use of my freedom. If I use it well, in my turn becomes more 'good' as a result, the good I have accomplished has a positive influ-ence on those around me" (John Paul II, *Memory and Identity*, 37).

101. Gutierrez, *Theology of Liberation*, 85. "Trasformazione dei sentimenti e delle passioni" (Grun, *Il coraggio di trasformarsi*, 40–44).

102. Gutierrez also speaks about the universalisation of the presence of God: from being localized and linked to a particular people it gradually extends to all people of the earth (*Theology of Liberation*, 87).

103. *Catechism of the Catholic Church* 1325. "Ignatius [of Antioch] calls the Eucha-rist, 'the medicine of immortality, the antidote against death, and everlasting life in Jesus Christ'" (Quasten, *Patrology*, 1:66).

104. *Catechism of the Catholic Church* 1333–34.

what you have with others, for such are the sacrifices which God approves" (Heb 13:16). *Koinonia* is a concrete gesture of human charity. Thus Paul uses this word to designate the collection organized on behalf of the Christians in Jerusalem; the Corinthians glorify God of their "liberation contribution to their need and to the general good" (2 Cor 9:13). Second, *koinonia* designates the union of the faithful with Christ through the Eucharist: "When we bless 'the cup of blessing,' is it not a means of sharing in the blood of Christ? When we break the bread, is it not a means of sharing in the union body of Christ?" (1 Cor 10:16). And third, *koinonia* means the union of Christians with the Father—"if we claim to be sharing in his life while we walk in the dark, our words and our lives are a lie" (1 John 1:6)—with the Son—"It is God himself who calls you to share in the life of his Son" (1 Cor 1:9)—and with the Spirit—"The grace of the Lord Jesus Christ, and the love of God, and fellowship in the Holy Spirit, be with you all" (2 Cor 13:14).[105]

During our lives, human beings have to discern between the "wheat" and the "weed" (Matt 13:24–30). However, it is only at the end of history, the *eschaton*, that the "harvest" will take place when sin will be totally eliminated. As Pope John Paul II states: "Evil is always the absence of some good which ought to be present in a given being; it is a privation."[106] Until that time Christians are invited to live in a *temporal dynamic spiral*, meaning they lead a decent life discerning their intentions and their deeds in their heart of hearts with a view to forming a better world where justice and peace reign. In our days the presence of missionaries is only a witness in order to see the spiritual needs of communities without ignoring their cultural and their temporal needs. Theologians and Saints provide us with profound spiritual teachings on how to lead a Christian life. One of these teachings is based on the Holy Spirit, who works with creation according to God's plan for our salvation.

105. Gutierrez, *Theology of Liberation,* 150.
106. John Paul II, *Memory and Identity,* 3.

Conclusion

The Power of Allegory

In this book importance is attached to the power of allegory, as a literary form, to describe and communicate what is significant in one's life. In the case of Hannah's narrative the episode of her daily life (chap. 2) and her knowledge of the Bible (chap. 3) formed the basis on which she allegorically constructed an ideal world. Through the tool of allegory she embodied her beliefs pertaining to her faith. What she could not express literally she easily expressed metaphorically. However, readers have to bear in mind that behind any allegorical narrative there is a human agent who could err in some respects.

Allegory does help individuals to share their knowledge, but it helps both readers and author relate with each other in their experiences even more. Readers are exposed to an ideal imaginary world constructed through the author's fertile imagination. However, they are in a position to question what it is being presented not only through rational thinking but also through their own affections and imagination. Their critical reflection first lies in their imagination but later through their reasoning. Allegory is a powerful literary tool at the disposal of the author; it connects author and readers through a mental and logical connection but also through affection and imagination. If allegory is employed cleverly it would not only stimulate the imagination of the reader but also create a relationship.

BEYOND HINDS' FEET ON HIGH PLACES

Hannah's spiritual merits, as depicted in the allegorical narrative, provide readers with the opportunity to ponder on their relationship with God. It is a spirituality that arises from an encounter with God and inspires readers to imitate Christ. The narrative's key value is that through the affective domain individuals come into contact with God's salvation in their lived experiences. In fact this spirituality is both a cry for authentic freedom and a means of reaching a better understanding of God. Only after such genuine experience can human beings undergo a transformation, a transformation which gradually adjusts the individual's way of thinking and actions to be in harmony with God's will. It also instils the desire into readers to seek God in every situation, even in situations which are envisaged as contradictory. Moreover, Hannah's spirituality encourages readers to dedicate themselves to a life of prayer and to cultivate a relationship with God which is rooted in sacred Scripture.

However, in Hannah's spirituality one finds many limitations. Her spirituality gives particular attention to the aspect of the human being. Moreover, it is a spirituality which is founded on a dualistic concept between body and spirit, world and God. These convictions not only distort an authentic Christian spirituality but affect individuals' relations toward others. No real spirituality exists unless there is harmony between the senses and the spirit. Adopting such an attitude could lead to a zealous lifestyle cut off from God's true plan for humanity. The salvation of this kind of spirituality does not treat people from different background at the same level, particularly in their mutual relationships, and disregards the fact that every person, no matter what kind of life one leads, has his own dignity.

Therefore, it is recommended that while embracing the spiritual merits of Hannah, one should also explore other Christian spiritualties which embrace harmony between human nature and God's will. This could be achieved through the active participation in religious activities, rites, and functions, such as the sacraments. These activities provide a sacred space in the profane world for people to assemble together and experience God. It also proposes that one should be acquainted with the knowledge and counsel handed over by exemplary people, who through their daily experiences impart to us how one can enhance faith during one's life.

This work also recommends that individuals who are seriously seeking to lead a life "according to the Spirit" (Rom 8:4) seek spiritual direction. Through spiritual direction one not only shares one's spiritual experiences with a spiritual director but also receives counsel to strengthen one's faith.

The spiritual director, who is a knowledgeable person in matters relating to the Spirit of God, enhances discernment. Through discernment the individual reflects on the feelings and relations with the world, thereby seeking to act according to God's will. Although this is a challenging process, his hope is to be in harmony with himself and the people around him. It is not an easy matter when one has to face feelings and problems. It is not a matter of feeling positive or feeling negative. Discernment questions both feelings because they are rooted in the individual's spirit. Hence these feelings derive their importance when they are related to our humanity. Otherwise they are of no significance. Christians require a sort of intelligence to discern emotions. Feelings act as signals which in turn lead to understanding oneself. By being responsible to one's own feelings the Christian becomes an active agent of freedom, a freedom which is founded on our fragile human nature but respected by God. Our God is not a God of feelings but a God of truth. Only by immersing in one's own prayers and through contemplation does one find the solutions. The voice which originates from the conscience gives us direction and leads us to our authentic meaning of life. Whatever the conscience utters should be discussed with the spiritual director as to whether these utterings coheres with God's Spirit. It is not a matter of receiving an answer ready made from others but listening to different trustworthy and knowledgeable counsel.

Unlike Much-Afraid's journey, our journey is not ready made and designed but involves different paths to reach the High Places or otherwise. Our desires should help us choose the best path to fulfil God's will in every aspect of our daily life. The Christian is faced with different paths of life to follow. In deciding which path to follow the individual should find that equilibrium which is in harmony with one's own humanity as God desires.

To reach a decision is not a simple task since it involves some risks, which in turn could lead to mistakes on our part. But this is how one expresses love toward God, and the way God instructs humanity. Through a leap in faith, one truly experiences God's love and mercy. Unlike Much-Afraid, to be forgiven by God is a real experience to us. Forgiveness is neither the result of one's actions and deeds accomplished for God nor the result of one's faith in Jesus in a profane world. Above all, forgiveness is a personal experience knowing that God, through his sheer mercy, forgave us. In turn this experience encourages us to seek God in all situations.

Through our decisions to act according to his will, we try to please God and not jeopardise in any way the loving bond with Christ. When one lives up to his faith, one hopes that one's actions yield positive results through the intervention and grace of God.

Bibliography

PRIMARY SOURCES

Hannah Hurnard's Writings

Hurnard, Hannah. *Eagles' Wings to the Higher Places*. New York: HarperCollins, 1981.
———. *Hearing Heart*. London: Church Mission to Jews, 1952.
———. *Hinds' Feet on High Places*. Carol Stream, IL: Tyndale, 1975.
———. *Kingdom of Love*. Carol Stream, IL: Tyndale, 1973.
———. *Mountains of Spices*. Carol Stream, IL: Tyndale, 1977.
———. *Steps to the Kingdom*. New York: HarperCollins, 1959.
———. *The Inner Man*. London: Powage, 1959.
———. *Thou Shalt Remember: Lessons of a Lifetime*. New York: HarperCollins, 1988.
———. *Walking among the Unseen*. Carol Stream, IL: Tyndale, 1982.
———. *Watchmen on the Walls*. Nashville: Broadman & Holman, 1997.
———. *Wayfarer in the Land*. Carol Stream, IL: Tyndale, 1981.
———. *Winged Life*. Carol Stream, IL: Tyndale, 1982.

Studies on Hannah Hurnard and Intertextuality

Anders, Isabel. *Standing on High Places: The Story of Hannah Hurnard*. Carol Stream, IL: Tyndale, 1994.
Allen, Graham. *Intertexuality*. London: Routledge, 2000.
De Lubac, Henri. *History and Spirit: The Understanding of Scripture according to Origen*. San Francisco: Ignatius, 2007.
Orr, Mary. *Intertexuality: Debates and Contexts*. Cambridge: Polity, 2003.
Wood, John. *Hannah Hurnard: The Authorized Biography: The Story behind the Spiritual Classic* Hinds' Feet on High Places. London: Monarch, 1997.

SECONDARY SOURCES

Magisterium

Benedict XVI. *Verbum Domini: The Word of God in the Life and Mission of the Church.* New York: Word among Us, 2010.

———. "Current Crisis Not Only Economic but Also Cultural and Spiritual." In *L'Osservatore Romano*, Vatican City, June 2, 2010, 1, 3.

Catechism of the Catholic Church. Washington, DC: USCCB, 1995.

John Paul II. *Memory and Identity: Personal Reflections.* London: Rizzoli, 2005.

———. *The Interpretation of the Bible in the Church.* Boston: Pauline Books & Media, 1993.

Vatican Council II. *Dei Verbum, Gaudium et spes, Lumen Gentium.* Boston: Pauline Books & Media, 1965.

Classics

Anthanasius. *Life of St. Antony.* NPNF[1] 4. Edited by Philip Schaff. Edinburgh: T&T Clark, 1892.

Augustine. *On Christine Doctrine.* NPNF[1] 14. Translated by J. J. Shaw. Edinburgh: T&T Clark, 1898.

———. *On Grace and Free Will: Retractions.* Translated by M. Inez Bogan. Washington, DC: Catholic University of America Press, 1968.

Da Capua, Raimondo. "La vita di St. Caterina di Siena." In *Esperienza e Spiritualita*, edited by Herbert Alphonso. Rome: Pomel, 2005.

De Caussade, Jean-Pierre. *Abandonment to Divine Providence.* San Francisco: Ignatius, 2008.

De Meester, Conrad. *With Empty Hands: The Message of St. Therese of Lisieux.* London: Burns & Oates, 2002.

de' Pazzi, Maria Maddalena. *I colloqui ii: Tutte le opere iii.* Edited by Claudio Catena. Firenze: Nerbini, 1963.

———. *I quaranta giorni: Tutte le opere i.* Edited by Claudio Catena. Firenze: Nerbini, 1960.

Gregory the Great. *Epistle to Theodorus.* NPNF[2] 12. Edited by Philip Schaff and Henry Wace. Peabody, MA: Hendrickson, 1995.

Gregory of Nyssa. *The Great Catechism.* NPNF[2] 5. Edited by Philip Schaff. Edinburgh: T&T Clark, 1892.

Hopkins, Jasper. *Nicholas of Cusa: De docta ignorantia.* Minneapolis: Arthur J. Banning, 1990.

Ignatius of Loyola. *The Autobiography.* Rev. ed. San Francisco: Ignatius, 2001.

———. *The Spiritual Exercises.* Translated by Elder Mullan. New York: Saint Benedict Press, 1914.

Irenaeus. *Against Heresies.* Translated by Henry Deane. Oxford: Clarendon, 2010.

John of the Cross. *A Spiritual Canticle of the Soul and the Bridegroom Christ.* Translated by David Lewis. London: Thomas Baker, 1919.

———. *Ascent of Mount Carmel.* Brewster, MA: Paraclete, 2008.

———. *Dark Night of the Soul.* Translated and edited by E. Allison Peers. New York: Image, 1994.

———. *The Collected Works of St. John of the Cross.* Translated by Kieran Kavanuagh and Otilio Rodriguez. Kalamazoo, MI: Institute of Carmelite Studies, 1991.

———. *The Poems of Saint John of the Cross.* Translated by Willis Barnstone. New York: W. W. Norton, 1972.

Origen. *De principiis.* Translated by Rufinus. ANF 4. Edinburgh: T&T Clark, 1892.

———. *The Song of Songs: Commentary and Homilies.* ACW 26. Translated by R. P. Lawson. Mahwah, NJ: Paulist Press, 1952.

———. *The Philokalia of Origen.* Translated George Lewis. Edinburgh: T&T Clark, 1911.

Otto, Rudolph. *The Idea of the Holy: An Inquiry into the Non Rational Factor in the Idea of the Divine.* Translated by John W. Harvey. Oxford: Oxford University Press, 1926.

Ponticus, Evagrius. *Praktikos.* Edited by Simon Tugwell. Oxford: Oxford University Press, 1987.

Quasten, Johannes. *Patrology: The Beginnings of Patristic Literature from the Apostles Creed to Irenaeus.* 4 vols. Notre Dame: University of Notre Dame Press, 1949–78.

Song of Songs: A New Translation with a Commentary, Anthologized from Talmud, Midrashic, and Rabbinic Sources. New York: Mesorah, 2010.

Teresa de Jesus. *Libro de la Vida 33/14: Obras completas.* Edited by Efren de la Madre de Dios and Otger Steggink. Madrid: BAC, 2003.

Teresa of Avila. *The Interior Castle, or the Mansions.* Translated by the Benedictines of Stanbrook. London: Thomas Baker, 1921.

The First Epistle of Clement to the Corinthians. ANF 1. Edited by Philip Schaff. Edinburgh: T&T Clark, 1892.

Xavier, Leon-Defour. "Muntanja." *Temi Biblici.* Translated by Komunità Neo-Katekumenali. Malta, 2002.

Others

Aers, David. *Piers Plowman and Christian Allegory.* London: E. Arnold, 1975.

All Nations Training Mission: http://www.allnations.ac.uk/ [April 6, 2011].

Aschenbrenner, George A. *Quickening the Fire in Our Midst.* Chicago: Loyola, 2002.

Astell, Ann W. *The Song of Songs in the Middle Ages.* Ithaca, NY: Cornell University Press, 1990.

Aumann, Jordan. *Spiritual Theology.* London: T&T Clark, 2001.

Barth, Karl. *Evangelical Theology: An Introduction.* Grand Rapids: Eerdmans, 1963.

Barthes, Roland. *Elements of Semiology.* London: Hill and Wang, 1984.

Beck, Edward L. *Soul Provider: Spiritual Steps to Limitless Love.* New York: Doubleday, 2007.

Bernard, Charles Andre. *Il Dio dei mistici: Le vie dell' interiorita.* Milan: San Paolo, 1996.

———. *Il dio dei mistici II: La conformazione a Cristo.* Milan: San Paolo, 1996.

———. *Teologia mistica.* Milan: San Paolo, 2005.

———. *Teologia spiritual.* Milan: San Paolo, 2002.

Benedict XVI. *Jesus of Nazareth.* 2 vols. San Francisco: Ignatius, 2007–11.

Bezzina, Joseph. *Methodology: A Style Manual for the Writing of Term Papers, Dissertations, and Theses.* Victoria-Gozo, 2005.

Brenner, A. *The Song of Songs.* Sheffield: Sheffield Academic Press, 1989.

Bibliography

Bunyan, John. *Pilgrim's Progress*. Harmondsworth: Penguin, 2008.

Burke, Patricia A. "The Healing Power of the Imagination." *International Journal of Children's Spirituality* 4, no. 1 (1999): 9–17.

Camilleri, Charlò. *Union with God as Transformation in Beauty: A Literary-Spiritual Analysis of the Colloquies of Santa Maria Maddalena de' Pazzi (1566–1607)*. Rome: Carmelitane, 2008.

———. *Carmel: A Spirituality of Beauty*. Malta, 2002.

Chodorow, Joan. *Jung on Active Imagination*. Princeton: Princeton University Press, 1997.

CMJ Israel: http://www.cmj-israel.org/Home.aspx [April 6, 2011].

Costanza, Bruna. *Abramo e l'esperienza della fede: In esperienza e spiritualita*. Edited by Herbert Alphonso. Rome, 2005.

De Man, Paul. *Allegories of Reading: Figural Language in Rousseau, Nietzsche, Rilke, and Proust*. New Haven: Yale University Press, 1979.

Downey, Michael. *Understanding Christian Spirituality*. Mahwah, NJ: Paulist Press, 1997.

Dawson, David. "Plato's Soul and the Body of the Text in Philo and Origen." In *Interpretation and Allegory*, edited by Jon Whitman. Boston: Brill, 2003.

Durham, Geoffrey. *The Spirit of the Quakers*. New Haven: Yale University Press, 2010.

Eliade, Mircea. *Patterns in Comparative Religion*. Translated by Rosemary Sheed. London: Sheed & Ward, 1996.

Farley, Margaret A. *A Framework for Christian Sexual Ethics*. London: Continuum, 2006.

Farrugia, Joanne. *Should Spirituality Lead to a Personal Relationship with God? A Christian Perspective*. Malta, 2008.

Fellowship for Evangelizing Britain's Villages: http://www.febv.org.uk/ [April 6, 2011].

Fisher, G. Richard. *From High Places to Heresy*: http://www.pfo.org/high-pla.html [April 6, 2011].

Fletcher, Agnus. *Allegory: The Theory of a Symbolic Mode*. Ithaca, NY: Cornell University Press, 1964.

Fodor, James. *Christian Hermeneutics: Paul Ricoeur and the Refiguring of Theology*. Oxford: Oxford University Press, 1995.

Fowler, James W. *Stages of Faith: The Psychology of Human Development and the Quest for Meaning*. New York: Harper, 1995.

Frye, Northrop. *Anatomy of Criticism: Four Essays*. Toronto: University of Toronto Press, 1957.

Gay, Clifford. *The Transformations of Allegory*. London: Routledge, 1974.

Gray, Madeleine. *The Protestant Reformation: Beliefs and Practices*. Sussex: Sussex Academic Press, 2003.

Grun, Anselm. *Il coraggio di trasformarsi: Alla scoperta del dinamismo della vita interiore*. Milan: San Paolo, 1999.

Golka, Friedemann W. *Revelation of God: A Commentary on the Books of the Song of Songs and Jonah*. Grand Rapids: Eerdmans, 1988.

Gordis, Robert. *The Song of Songs and Lamentations: A Study, Modern Translation, and Commentary*. New York: Ktav, 1974.

Gula, Richard M. *The Call to Holiness: Embracing a Fully Christian Life*. Mahwah, NJ: Paulist Press, 2003.

Gutierrez, Gustavo. *We Drink from Our Own Wells: The Spiritual Journey of a People*. Maryknoll, NY: Orbis, 2005.

———. *A Theology of Liberation*. Maryknoll, NY: Orbis, 2009.

Hein, Rolland. *Christian Mythmakers*. Chicago: Cornerstone, 2002.

James, William. *The Varieties of Religious Experience: A Study in Human Nature*. New York: Library of America, 2008.

Johnston, Andrew. *The Protestant Reformation in Europe: Seminar Studies in History*. Philadelphia: Trans-Atlantic, 1991.

Julia, Kristeva. *Desire in Language: A Semiotic Approach to Literature and Art*. New York: Columbia University Press, 1980.

Kelly, Francis. "Through the Church Year." In *L'Osservatore Romano*, Vatican City, June 2, 2010, 6.

Kelly, Geffrey B., ed. *Karl Rahner: Theologian of the Graced Search for Meaning*. Minnepolis: Fortress, 1992.

King, J. Christopher. *Origen on the Song of Songs as the Spirit of Scripture: The Bridegroom's Perfect Marriage-Song*. Oxford: Oxford University Press, 2009.

Lewis, C. S. *The Allegory of Love: A Study in Medieval Tradition*. Oxford: Oxford University Press, 1959.

Ludlow, Morwenna. "Theology and Allegory: Origen and Gregory of Nyssa on the Unity and Diversity of Scripture." *International Journal of Systematic Theology* 4, no. 1 (2002): 45–66.

MacQueen, John. *Allegory*. London: Methuen, 1970.

Moore, W. J. *Christ, the Church, and the Soul*. London: Burns & Oates, 1961.

Mountain, Vivienne. "Educational Contexts for the Development of Children's Spirituality: Exploring the Use of Imagination." *International Journal of Children's Spirituality* 12, no. 2 (2007): 191–205.

Orsuto, Donna. *Holiness*. London: Continuum, 2006.

Piehler, Paul. *The Visionary Landscape: A Study in Medieval Allegory*. London: Edward Arnold, 1972.

Quaker Spirituality: Selected Writings. Edited by Emilie Griffin and Douglas V. Steere. New York: HarperCollins, 2005.

Quilligan, Maureen. *The Language of Allegory: Defining the Genre*. Ithaca, NY: Cornell University Press, 1979.

Radcliffe, Timothy. *What Is the Point of Being a Christian?* London: Burns & Oates, 2006.

Ricoeur, Paul. *Figuring the Sacred: Religion, Narrative, and Imagination*. Minneapolis: Fortress, 1995.

Robertson, D. W. *A Preface to Chaucer: Studies in Medieval Perspectives*. Princeton: Princeton University Press, 1962.

Stone, Bryan. *Evangelism after Christendom: The Theology and Practice of Christian Witness*. Grand Rapids: Brazos, 2007.

Tambling, Jeremy. *Allegory*. London: Routledge, 2010.

Tanner, Norman P. *The Church and the World: Gaudium et spes, Inter mirifica*. Mahwah, NJ: Paulist Press, 2005.

Thiselton, Anthony C. *Hermeneutics: An Introduction*. Grand Rapids: Eerdmans, 2009.

Tugwell, Simon. *Way of Imperfection: An Exploration of Christian Spirituality*. London: Darton, Longman & Todd 1985.

Ward, Graham. "Allegoria: Reading as a Spiritual Exercise." *Modern Theology* 15, no. 3 (1999): 288–89.

Walter, Benjamin. *The Origin of German Tragic Drama*. London: Verso, 1998.

Whitman, Jon. *Allegory: The Dynamics of an Ancient and Medieval Technique*. Oxford: Clarendon, 1987.

Zammit, Emmanuel. *Men's Call to Holiness: An Aspect of Pauline Spirituality*. Malta, 2006.

Subject/Name Index

Made in the USA
Middletown, DE
04 April 2016